Armand Eeckels and Halewijn Lievens explored the works, ideas and ambitions of NU architectuuratelier in an eight-hour recording which formed the basis for this book.
/ Feb. 2023 at the NU architectuuratelier office (together with Bertrand Lafontaine)

exploring
NU architectuuratelier

Verlag der Buchhandlung
Walther und Franz König, Köln

A+ Architecture in Belgium

Bozar

Foreword
Emma Filippides and Ben Rea
p. 7

Explorations
Armand Eeckels and Halewijn Lievens
p. 9 – 156

**Will it be very light or will it
be very heavy?**
Stefan Devoldere
p. 160 - 171

12 projects
p. 172 - 212

Project list
p. 215 - 218

Bio
p. 219

FOREWORD
Emma Filippides and Ben Rea

'Imagine that you arrive somewhere in the middle of a forest. There are two big rocks in your path and a tree has fallen down nearby. If you had to start organizing the space, these three basic elements would naturally guide your approach to its organization. You would also have to think of a way to make it your own, to translate these elements into a meaningful use.' [1]

It is interesting to think about architecture as an assembly of individual objects, each with their own internal logic, offering opportunities for improvisation and juxtaposition. Suddenly, something which could easily be considered temporary or impermanent can become something more significant, perhaps even the foundation of a building. A single element –plinth, table, clearing, terrain – can act as an anchor around which activity can centralize, a point of ritual intensity.

NU's interest in the elemental experience of architecture frees the practice from referential constraints, focusing instead on an individual's experience as the starting point for design. NU's investigations are rooted in the feeling of the body in space, the feeling of the body in relation to others, and the feeling of the body in adjacency to building. A restless curiosity in 'use' and the quality of spatial experience fuels NU's search for original solutions and the experimental pursuit of untested ideas. It is an architecture that is situated in the present; it both recognizes the immediacy of the moment and anticipates the next.

NU's knowledge of building and making things, acquired from their earliest 1:1 experiments, continues to find root in the work of the office. The immediacy and uncertainty of the process provokes an open and questioning attitude towards design development. The result is work that blurs the distinction between furniture and building. For NU, architecture is a way to make contact with the immediate human scale and question how people interact with and use things. When this 1:1 fascination with the individual experience of architecture is translated into NU's work, pieces of furniture take on an architectural meaning while the city itself becomes pliable like furniture. As the office has grown, it is with this original interest that NU has approached larger architectural projects and master plans.

Many of life's rituals grew out of the most humble and functional of considerations, and yet the word 'ritual' speaks to something far deeper than function alone. NU's process flows similarly through echoing connections between one thing and another, approached with an attitude free of prejudice and full of curiosity and care.

In 2020 Emma and Ben were invited by Armand and Halewijn to embark upon a research collaboration with NU to reflect upon and articulate the office's work, process and internal culture. Through an open and searching process which continued until 2022, Emma and Ben sought to uncover the connections and inspirations at the heart of NU and the many authors, questions and experiments that comprise NU's approach to architecture.

[1] Text adapted from a dialogue between Armand Eeckels, Halewijn Lievens, Emma Filippides and Ben Rea.

To ask questions and explore. To bluff and cash in. To look into new connections and meanings, new materials and new ways of combining programmes. We aim to stand in the world and play.

To realize our first project in Halvemaanstraat in Ghent (2003), we ourselves hammered together the formwork for the kitchen and poured the concrete. This was the start of a search for what we wanted to work on, for what NU architectuuratelier could be. /1 2 3

 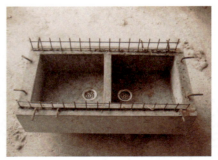

Instead of creating a delimited space, we made a concise kitchen unit that starts from its use. The actions of dining and cooking come together in a rough concrete element. An unyielding piece of furniture that stands in the way a little.
/ 4

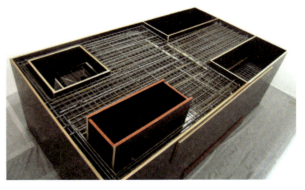

The Flanders Architecture Institute invited us to participate in the exhibition series *35m³ young architecture* (2006). For this, we remade the formwork of the kitchen. It was a 're-enactment', a reliving of the decisive moment that shaped our way of working (together). The power and beauty of the formwork are what fascinate us in the intermediate phase of a creative process. / 5

Every time we ourselves made furniture pieces for a project, we would close the drawing office for a week, put all our tools in the car, drive to the site and camp nearby. Here we hammered away at the wooden formwork for three days. On day four, we bound the reinforcement. On the fifth day, we poured the concrete mass into the formwork, and that evening we started polishing the surface. We saw the concrete pulp harden and become an immovable mass, ready to be used, ready to take on meaning. / 6

When we make things, we take it as seriously as young kids building a camp. / 7

Every detail matters. Slowed down, focused. There is no yesterday, there is no tomorrow. There is only the here and now. A full engagement in the moment.
/ 8 Zinalrothorn, Switzerland

Our bird lookout at the Bellefroid ponds near Leuven (2021) is architecture for fauna and flora. Humans are only guests there. They can watch but without disturbing. / 9

We explore the soil that has always been under our feet as a building material. We work with earth and materials that are present in the environment and that nature can spontaneously attach to. As a landscape for sheltered viewing, it is in the first place a catalyst for biodiversity. / 10 masterplan in collaboration with Overlant

When humans let go of a built structure and hand it over to the laws of nature, a new and powerful landscape emerges. A symbiosis between the vestige and its surroundings.

/ 11 From: Jean-Claude Gautrand, *Forteresses du dérisoire* (Les Presses de la Connaissance, 1977)

Erosion and degradation are the driving forces of the bird lookout. With the passing of time – nobody knows how long exactly – the structure will erode and take on an increasingly random shape. Ultimately, there will only be landscape.
/ 12

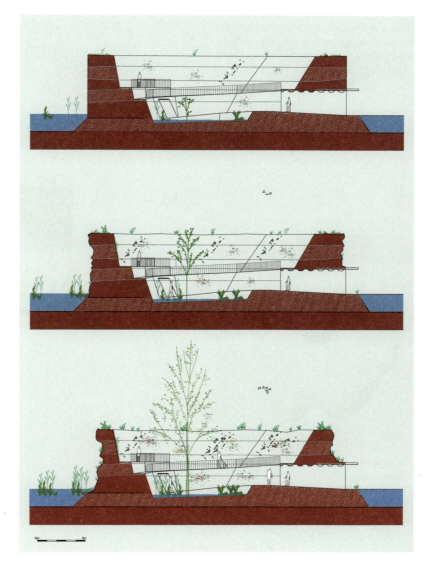

The inquisitive, process-based, adventurous spirit of the early years is something we still cherish in our current architectural practice. We never start from a preconceived plan but set off on a journey, engage in inspiring discussions with other experts, step by step and with advancing insight. / 13

Protected viewing. The bunker's formal language follows directly from its dual function. The expressive architecture you experience physically flows from the functional logic of the structure.

/ 14 From: Paul Virilio, *Bunker Archeology* (2009)

We suppress expectations of what a bird lookout should look like. The formal language stems from a 'bio-logic' we apply throughout the project. It is not necessary to add an aesthetic statement.

/ 15 Skeleton of a sea urchin

How do you design a bath for two? By digging a hole in the sand on the beach. The fine sand allows you to precisely define the space around your body. It is an immediate and corporeal way of thinking and designing.
/ 16 In collaboration with Stefanie Everaert

Digging led to a bath with an amorphous shape. You can sit side by side or opposite one another, and there is room for a couple of glasses on the edge … / 17 18

The monolithic architecture of the small church Biete Giyorgis in Ethiopia was created by removing rather than adding rock. Freeing what is already there, un-covering. The work is contained in the void. / 19

For the living and gallery space above Canadian artist Royden Rabinowitch's studio in Ghent, we made two models showing the same spaces. One with positive (full) volumes and one with negative (empty) volumes. The living area and the gallery are intertwined by stairs that never cross. / 20

This model gives shape to the light and space concept, like an autonomous sculpture. / 21

/ 22 Royden Rabinowitch, *Untitled*, S.M.A.K., Ghent, 2001

Architecture often has an enveloping, protective function. Being in such a space is a fundamental physical experience of the niche.
/ 23 Henry Moore, *Helmet Head No. 1*, 1950 (cast 1960), bronze on wood base

For a Steiner school in Ghent (2019), we introduced a space as a protective shell in which children can act, play music and move freely. / 24

The different spaces of the primary school are conceived as loose stones in rushing water between which the children's outdoor play can freely flow. Breaking away from conditioned, orthogonal thinking, the organic lines in the design create a lively dynamic. / 25

As the plot was relatively small for the programme and we wanted to keep a lot of outdoor space, we proposed a pragmatic stacking of functions with different levels and horizons, like decks on a passenger ship. / 26

A typology of function and experience, of both machine and architecture. / 27 28

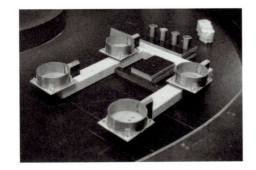

To shape the ritual of cooking on a fire in its essence, we cast the gas burners directly into the concrete work surface. We dismantled a standard gas cooker, placed the burners further apart, and made a detailed, machine-like hollow for it in the formwork.
/ 29

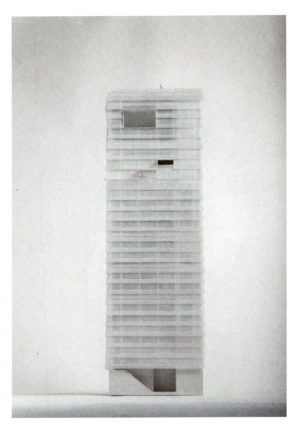 

Stacking according to the logic of the programme forms the design of a temporary info tower on Rooseveltplaats in Antwerp (2014). We anchored a tall, vertical, demountable steel skeleton with a translucent skin on a massive base of concrete blocks.
The scaled façade protects the stacked programme from rain and offers strategic views over the square and the city.
/ 30 31

By stacking programmes precisely, you tell a certain story, you trace a scenographic walk. / 32

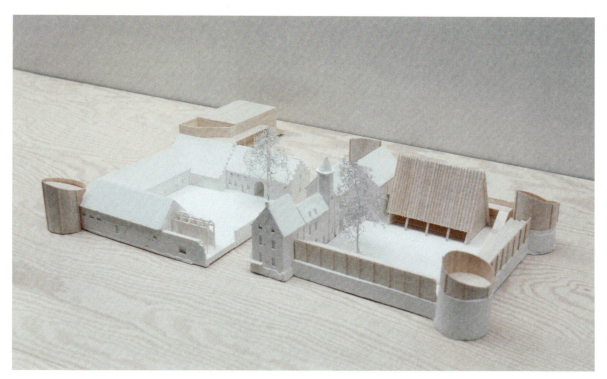

For the conversion of a medieval commandry in Gruitrode into a visitor centre (2022), we turned to historical documents for inspiration: for example, a text describing in detail a dinner in the banquet hall. Different architectural interventions lend themselves to telling the historical story of the site and the landscape around it.

/ 33 In collaboration with Michel Janssen arch. (restauration) & Kabvis (scenography)

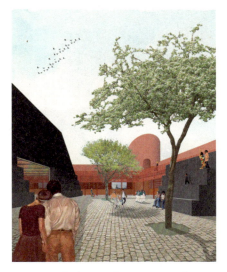

We not only designed a tourist product, but also created a place for the community of Gruitrode, a place for gatherings and encounters, events and fairs. The added social commitment to the assignment for a tourist programme is essential for the sustainable development of a historic place. / 34

Our interpretation of the Mundus building from Pieter Jan Bouman's 1953 *Revolutie der eenzamen* (Revolution of the lonely) is a black, spherical mausoleum. Mourners in procession pay their respects to Lenin on the Red Square in Moscow (1924).
/ 35 Christophe Gerrewey, *50 fictieve gebouwen* (Borgerhoff & Lamberigts, 2014)

The spherical shape as the most inert architecture.
/ 36 Kazimir Malevich, *Black Circle*, 1915, oil on canvas, State Russian Museum, St Petersburg, Russia

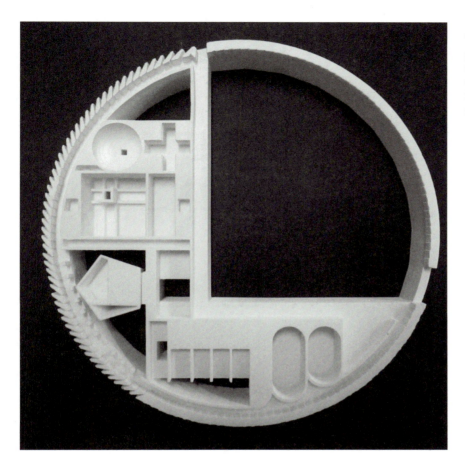

The circle is the smallest figure for a given programme, a form in which architecture disappears altogether. In our competition proposal for a crematorium in Zemst (2011), the circle describes the ritual of parting. / 37

The crematorium borders an industrial zone. Its circular shape makes it into a world in itself, with a context all its own. **Like an island.** / 38 Venice's cemetery on the island of San Michele

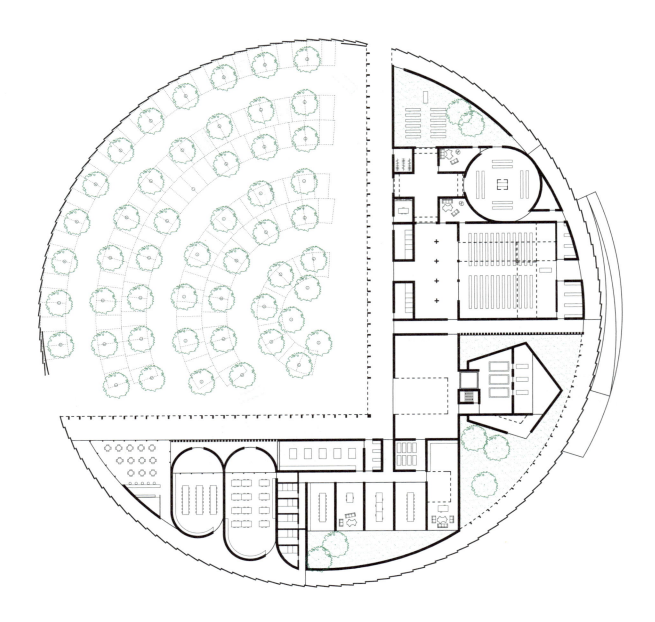

The mourners themselves string together different indoor and outdoor spaces with a different intimacy, scale and atmosphere into a personal farewell ritual. A ceremony which arriving and parking are already part of. / 39 40 41

In his search for the essence of the female head, Brancusi came closer and closer to the egg shape. The beginning of all life and a symbol of absolute beauty.
/ 42 Constantin Brancusi, *Le Commencement du monde*, 1920-24, Centre Pompidou, Paris

/ 43

In collaboration with Huis Perrekes in Oosterlo, a care home for people with dementia, we developed a cradle bed (2017). The cradle bed closes the circle of life, its beginning and end. / 44

This small sculpture of beeswax has been moulded in such a way as to rock both lengthwise and sidewise. We developed these two rocking directions for the cradle bed. Each has its own meaning and provides a different experience. / 45

Cradling is comforting. The Quakers left space in this rocking chair for a baby to sway to the rhythm of the person sitting next to it and rocking it to sleep. / 46

Cradling connects the one who cradles with the one who is cradled, and conversely. The movement is equally comforting for the one doing the rocking. The act of cradling is most powerful at the moment when a loved one takes their leave of someone at life's end in the cradle bed, while rocking. It gives meaning to the way we are here in this world as human beings.

The bed is a form of micro-architecture. It is a niche in which one can feel truly secure. A small, intimate universe, like the experiential world of persons with dementia in an advanced stage of the disease. / 47 Still from Ingel Vaikla's film on the cradle bed, 2018

During several trials at Huis Perrekes, we went in search of the right rhythm and the right rocking motion: rocking lengthwise, rocking sidewise, rocking in suspension. The cradle bed was made of pine plywood, an easy-to-work and modest material, like Arte Povera. The focus of the design isn't on materiality or detailing, but rather on the act of cradling, the connecting moment. / 48 49

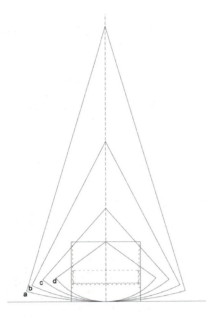
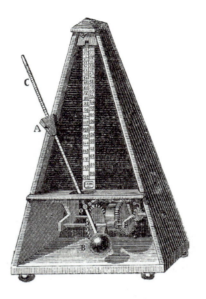
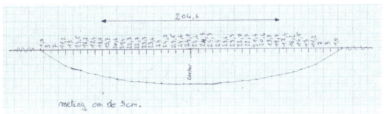

A large radius of curvature means faster rocking, while a small radius rocks more slowly. We studied meticulously the rhythm of rocking that brings comfort and calm. Finding the right geometric curvature for rocking is a matter of millimetres. / 50

The cradle bed has a mechanical lever that enables it to gradually be converted into a fixed bed that rests firmly on the floor. This is essential because getting into or waking up in a bed that is rocking or that is not completely stable can be frightening. / 51

When one of our team members became a proud father of a beautiful little girl, we designed a small version of the cradle bed that can easily be turned into a boat to play in, and built it ourselves with the team. / 52

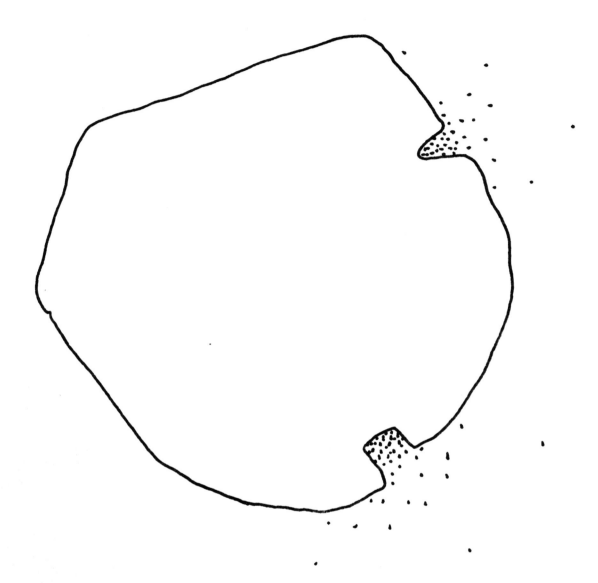

What does the boundary of the Meise Botanic Garden, one of the largest botanical gardens in the world, mean for the public domain around it? How could we retranslate, and charge with meaning, the boundary between public space and the enclosed garden? / 53

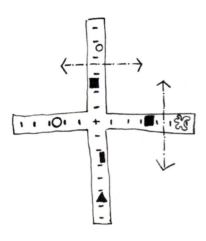

/ 54

We transformed what used to be a hard line between public and private, between inside and outside, into a boundary space that mediates and connects. The cruciform reception pavilion lets the public domain flow into the forecourt of the Botanic Garden. The cross orders and accommodates all reception functions in an exchange with the outdoor environment. / 55 56

The prefabricated, concrete T-structures stand in a well-defined grid. They form a series of abstracted trees. / 57

The new structure together, with young metasequoias, will flank the garden's main historic avenue. / 58

Where the landscape descends, the structure takes the form of a jetty, detached from the ground. / 59

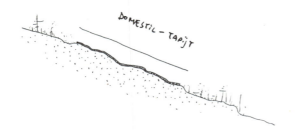

In the design of a house in Lierneux (2015), the pronounced slope of the site forms the domestic carpet for living. / 60

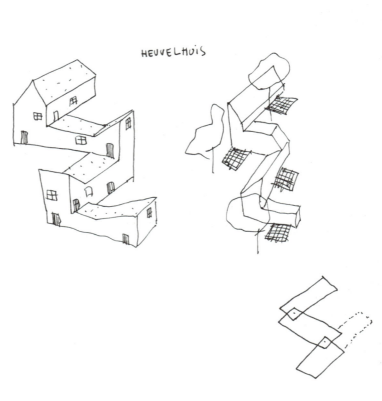

The slope in the landscape continues into the house. The floor heights climb along in terraces, while the ceiling height is extended horizontally. This creates rooms with very different heights and characters. / 61

More inspiring than thinking in terms of walls and rooms is to start from the landscape as a support which the different rituals of living can nestle on. / 62

On the Shetland Islands, the weather is windy, wet and harsh. The landscape is desolate, barren and fragile. In 2018 we were commissioned to convert a late medieval ruin on an estuary there into a small single-person home. / 63

According to the islanders, The Windhouse is inhabited by ghosts. The client's mission was to put to rest the spirits living there. As designers, we were challenged to look at the ruin, its history and living in this lonely place through a specific frame of reference. / 64

Various traces, some dating back to the Neolithic, remain eternal scars in the bleak landscape. Grave mounds, a broch (a kind of Iron Age circular stone tower found only in Scotland), here and there the remains of an ancient stone wall.
/ 65 66

The site has been listed by the authorities. Renovating is therefore roughly synonymous with reconstructing, restoring it to the original condition. But to what condition, from what period? / 67

The ruin turned out to be a former chapel, with a graveyard around it. Later, the chapel was converted into a dwelling. / 68

We left the ruin itself untouched. It became a cluster of walled garden rooms, where ravens live and the house pony finds shelter from fierce rain and wind. The process in which the ruin increasingly becomes the landscape can continue. A landscape of memories. / 69

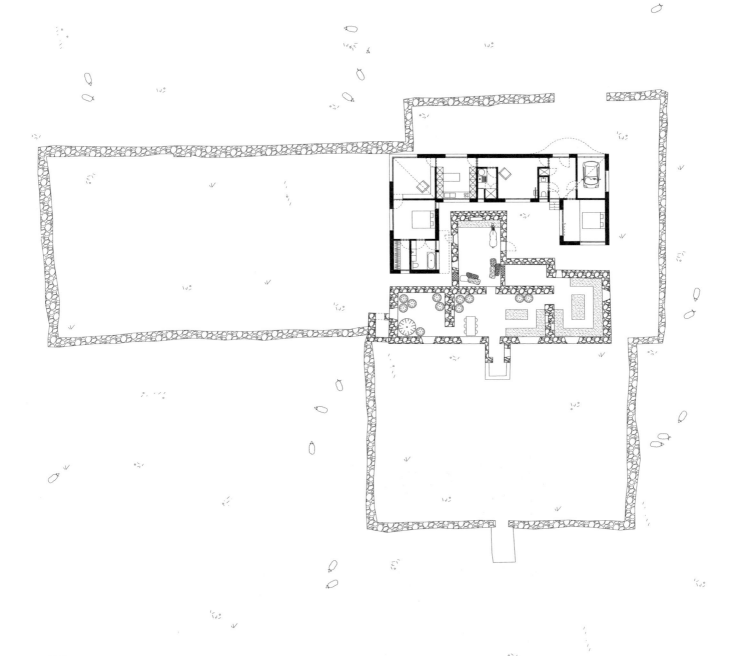

Our design gives expression to the mission of the client, as guardian and protector of spirits. We inserted a small, new residence into the back of the ruin, a guardhouse tailored to the woman's autarchic existence. The pony and the chicken lodges are situated in the ruin.

/ 70

Small domestic artefacts define our ability to remind ourselves what living is.
/ 71 Rachel Whiteread, *Vitrine Objects* (2010)

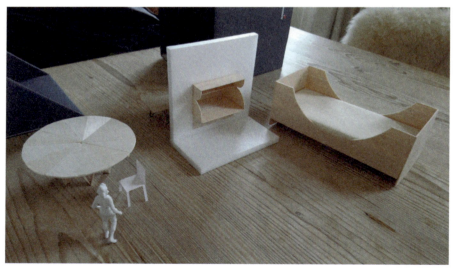

For Huis Perrekes, a home for people with dementia, we developed pieces of furniture which help to recall the essence of what living is: a bed, a table, a secretaire and some lamps. / 72

Like a new heart, the kitchen is centrally located along the large living rooms of Huis Perrekes's renovated doctor's villa. Homeliness lies not so much in the cosy decor as in community life and all the meaningful activities that follow. / 73

Just before noon, there is the smell of freshly made soup. And around four o'clock, the table is set for coffee. Dishes are washed and the laundry is folded. What could be more natural than cooking, preparing food, washing up – the day's rituals, setting the rhythm that provides the best grip for people with dementia? / 74

By making a kitchen yourself, you engage differently with the space and with the materials. You don't just look at a project through your computer, but are physically present in that space and experience it up close. When the kitchen for Hans and Joke in Wevelgem was finished, we cooked for them. / 75

At our office, lunch has evolved in such a way that every day two of us prepare food for everyone in turn. That has to do with slowing down, with 'living well'. We share a profession and work together, but there is actually more that connects us. / 76

And then we all sit around the table together. The table as a social space for dialogue on our common project. / 77

When King Philippe and Queen Mathilde visited Huis Perrekes, the round table proved too small for those in attendance. / 78

We had wooden circle segments made which can lie loose on that table so as to enlarge the circumference on festive occasions. A counterweight is then placed in the centre of the table to hold everything together. / 79

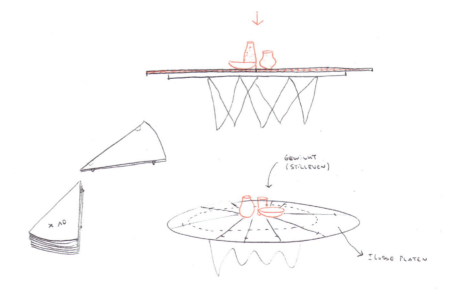

The still life composed of casted elements at the centre of the table is a gift we gave Huis Perrekes as a thank you for the instructive collaboration. / 80

The moulds for the still life are a collection of the finest everyday shapes from the Action supermarket. / 81

Whereas Apollo represents the static, balanced intellect and that which strives for measure, order and harmony, Dionysus represents the cycle of life, the impulsive and intuitive inner life. Problem-solving thinking contrasts with the capacity to care. In our architecture, in our partnership, both are present and are in a lasting relation marked by tension. / 82

Making these light-bricks was a unique and intensive process. Adventurous, but in controlled steps. On one side, Armand is following a line drawing, while on the other Halewijn is following another line drawing. This creates a surprising but correct shape. / 83

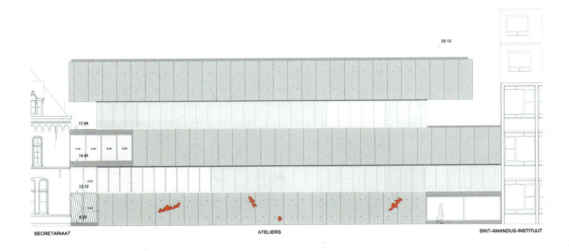

We created translucent moulds in the concrete street wall of the Sint-Lucas school of arts in Ghent. Openings based on the quirky shapes Xaveer De Geyter had drawn with chalk on a travertine limestone. / 84

To keep water that flows along the façade outside, the drawing of the inner façade is higher than the drawing in the concrete street façade. / 85

Each step was new and surprising but
had to be thought through to the end,
as there was no room for error.
We had to get it right the first time. / 86

The first step was to cut the quirky figures as a positive shape from blue foam using fuse wire.

The negative mould of silicone and reinforced laminate is then created around these moulds.

Moulds on a glass plate.

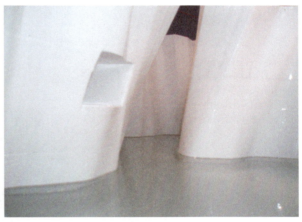

We poured the epoxy resin into these moulds. Every day for thirty days, we poured a 1 cm layer of transparent casting resin to avoid overheating.

The pieces were then removed from the moulds and mounted in a plywood board.

Finally, the pieces were mounted vertically in the formwork of the inner wall.

The reinforcement was woven around it, ready to place the outer formwork and pour highly liquid concrete around it. / 87

The result in itself is striking and modest at the same time. These are strange openings, like specks spilled on the concrete, but then with a certain depth, shiny sides and a particular light refraction. / 88

Openings without reference. / 89

In their flat in Amsterdam, Aldo and Hannie van Eyck placed a steel ring around a stove with a simple plank on top. Depending on how hot it is, you can draw the board closer or push it back. It is the expression of an obvious utility and forms a central space around the stove. / 91 Hannie and Aldo van Eyck, 1947

We often have campfire moments during our outings. Once darkness has fallen, we stare into the primitive fire together and sing songs. We try to use the same focus and ambition both in developing our architectural projects and in working together as a team. / 90

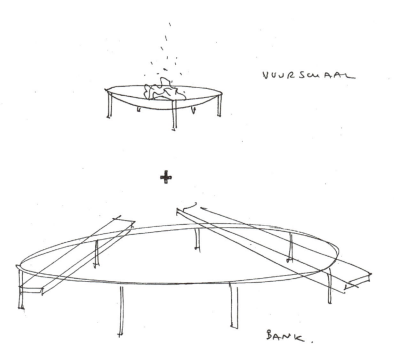

For the park-garden of Huis Perrekes, we developed this round bench. Loose beams determine the seating constellation in the circle. It is an ode to Hannie and Aldo van Eyck. / 92

A former water tower near Ichtegem was to become a lookout. But what if we turned that high plateau into a place you could stay for a while? / 93

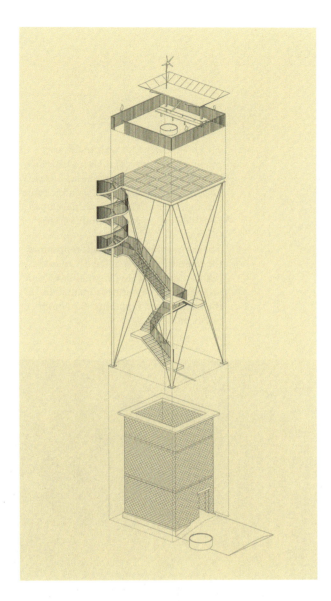

The shell of the water tower was preserved as a walled garden. That is where the stairs start, up to the edge of that walled area. And then you climb further and further until you reach the plateau overlooking the surrounding area. The tower's utilitarian expression follows from the logic of its use and construction.

By introducing a new use at the lookout such as picnicking or sitting at a table overlooking the expansive view, visitors get a richer experience of that place. They can slow down for a moment, be more present. Too often, lookouts offer only fleeting moments. / 94

The intensive logical translation of a function often produces talking objects, such as this device made for listening. Sheltered from the rain and wind, a person sitting in the small cabin with their ear to the giant funnel can hear for miles. Low tech, pure and simple.

/ 95 Giant ear trumpet for outer space, U.S. Bell Telephone System's space research laboratory at Holmdel (New Jersey), 1968

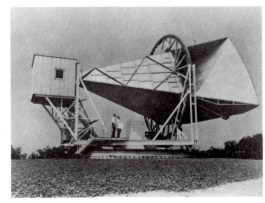

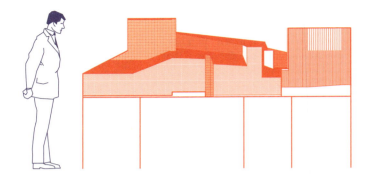

This model on a 1:40 scale of Concertgebouw Brugge (2017) is both a listening-installation and an instrument. It is part of Concertgebouw Circuit, a public route through the building that we developed in collaboration with Mathilde Geens (Kabvis).
The main volume on the left represents the majestic concert hall with an integrated pianoforte. In the smaller volume on the right, the more intimate sound of the harpsichord represents the chamber music hall. / 96 97

Together with furniture maker Luc Roose, we developed a machine, an instrument. When a visitor turns the horizontal flywheel, a rubber band is set in motion on which a music composition by Heleen van Haegenborgh has been 'written' in studs. This mechanism plays simultaneously both the converted pianoforte and the harpsichord strings.
/ 98 99 100

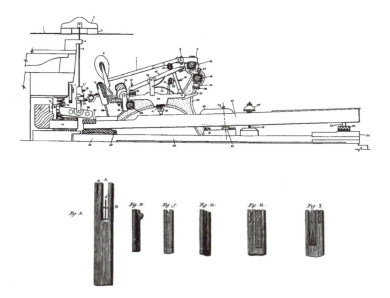

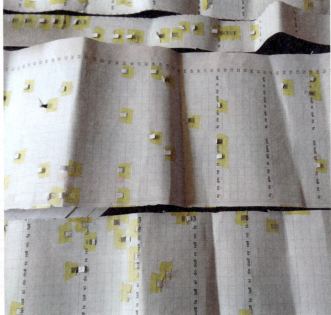

The formal logic of the skeleton of a cactus provided the botanical inspiration for the competition proposal for the Green Ark visitor pavilion at the Meise Botanic Garden. / 101

We explored how that form and the properties of wood could come together in a striking spatial structure with an accessible deck that also shades the place where you can see inside the surrounding greenhouses. / 102

The pavilion is nestled in a sea of glass-houses with climate zones from around the world. It is the treasury of living plants and seeds that the pavilion unlocks visually for the public.
/ 103 In collaboration with Archipelago

It is a mediating space, a link between the precious collection in its controlled climate and the public. / 104

The contractor made a scale model to conceive all the nodes and see how all the ribs descend on the horizontal deck.
/ 105 in collaboration with Mouton

The paraboloid rib structure is composed of thin, flexible planks up to 20 m long. When the planks are alternately nailed together like a weave, you obtain a rigid structure, which then transfers the forces of the tensioning structure to the paraboloid head walls. / 106 107

The iconic 1963 head frame at the Genk mining site was given a new lease of life by restoring to the gigantic steel tripod its load-bearing function. A long, suspended fyke with a spiral staircase takes visitors up to a height of 72 m, offering views of the surrounding landscape transformed by the mine. /108

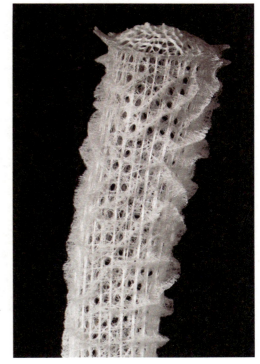

Glass sponges are the oldest living organisms, more than 9,000 years old. They are characterized by a skeleton consisting of four- and/or six-pointed spicules of silica (SiO_2). /109

The segments of the fyke are conceived as a light and rigid membrane open to the wind that requires the full height of the stairs to be connected to the head frame at only three points. / 110

We cherish the memory of assembling
this impressive infrastructure. / 111 112

The residents and staff of Huis Perrekes
made small lampshades together, crocheted from sheep's wool. / 113

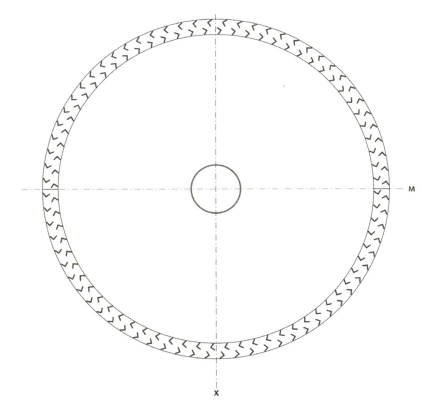

Our main objective along the Noord-Zuid infrastructure project in Limburg has been to look at the infrastructure not only as a product of engineering but as an architectural artefact, deeply rooted in the surrounding landscape. In this approach, improving connectivity leads to improving the liveability and sustainability of the areas impacted by the project. / 114 115 In collaboration with 51N4E and Maat-ontwerpers

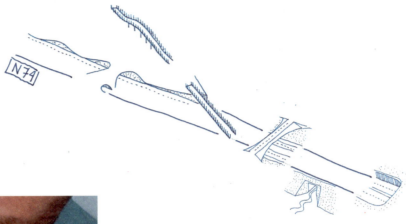

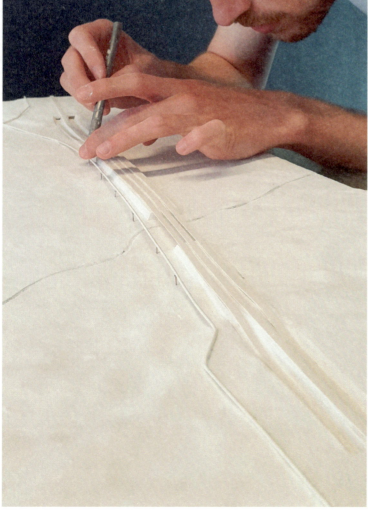

In this understanding, the regional road between Hasselt and Eindhoven transcends its two-dimensional character and becomes a spatial, contextual object within an intricate ecosystem, negotiating between the material detail and the large-scale infrastructure in the landscape, between the natural and the constructed, between human and non-human. / 116 117

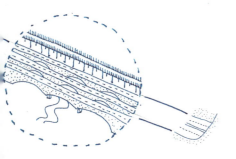

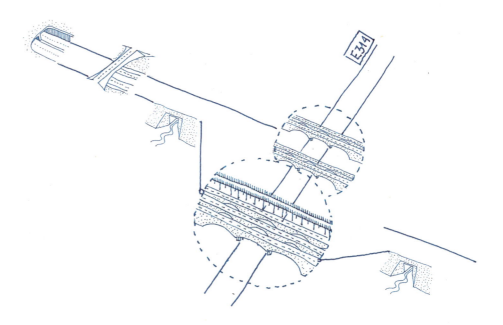

The Centers project consisted in repurposing the railway infrastructure in Borgerhout, which forms the boundary between residential areas and the large-scale infrastructure of the Antwerp ring road. / 118

The old railway arches formed a rear side, a dull boundary. / 119

The project provides a service. It is infrastructure for potential activation. / 120

Turning the sloping embankment at the back of the Centers arches into a stepped design, a useful ancillary space is created that can be put to different uses.
/ 121 122

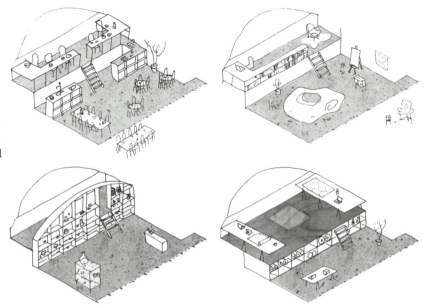

Together, the sixty arches form one infrastructure but, as separate small alcoves to the city, they are a great opportunity to revitalize this part of town and generate high-quality public space. As a 700 m linear infrastructure, their potential impact in this part of town is substantial.
/ 123 124

The Centers arches provide space for a wide range of initiatives and programmes, such as studios, shops, meeting places, a brewery, small catering establishments, bicycle storage, and so on.

The programme charges this urban boundary and the momentum of the various activities radiates into the public space that is regularly included in its use.
/ 125 126

Our office on the quay is a stone's throw from Gent-Dampoort railway station. We use this public space as our front garden, putting tables outside in the afternoon and having lunch together. We also use it for meetings or to have a break among people coming from the station and heading into town. / 127

Tempelhof, Berlin. An unforgettable day during an outing with our team. The wide-open space invites movement, strolling, play and interaction. It is a place where a lot of contact is possible, precisely because of its immense scale. Intimacy is created by the vastness of the space. / 128

Between Gent-Sint-Pieter railway station and the city centre lies Citadelpark, home to a cluster of buildings like a closed conglomerate. At its heart lies the Floraliënhal.
Freeing up this vast covered space and extending the park into it creates a unique meeting space for Ghent. For strolling, for small daily use and large activities. The openness of the Floraliënhal turns the surrounding park into a full-fledged space as a garden for the area. The new typology of the covered public space absorbs the urban dynamics and gives addresses to the surrounding functions such as the duplicated S.M.A.K. at the ends, the renovated International Convention Center Gent ICC and the indoor cycling track 't Kuipke.
/ 129 130 In collaboration with 51N4E

(next page)
Plan based on the Nolli drawings of Rome showing the public spaces. On the left is the railway station of Ghent, on the right is the Sint-Pietersplein. Central is the Citadelpark. / 131

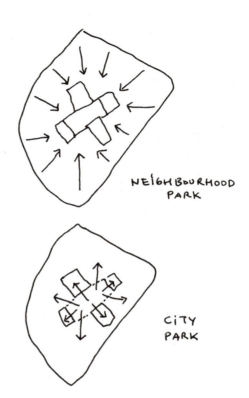

We imagine the Floraliënhal as a gigantic urban space whose scale makes it democratic and invites people to move, show, look and interact. As in Tempelhof, where an abundance of space again allows intimacy to emerge. / 132

Former Flemish Government Architect Peter Swinnen asked us to design a functional showcase that makes the operations of the Team Flemish Government Architect visible to the public. This workspace, the Atelier Bouwmeester, curves along the covered public space of the Ravenstein Gallery in Brussels, generating interaction with the public space that is at once spontaneous and strong. / 133

We translated the assignment into a collection of autonomous furniture pieces that divide the continuous space into different fields and gives each field a programme. Each furniture unit speaks from its own specific internal logic. The kitchen has been pushed invitingly against the gallery window. A large screen made of translucent corrugated sheets demarcates the kitchen. The kitchen cabinet is an open aluminium box against the wall. / 134

Projects regularly arise within projects. Separate components that are worked out autonomously only to come together again in a common space.
/ 135 Kazimir Malevich, Suprematism, *Two-dimensional Self-portrait*, 1915

Four bookcases rotate on their axes. Mobile panels hang for presentations and a curved curtain closes off a presentation room. / 136

/ 137 Concept image

We were commissioned to redefine the foyer of Concertgebouw Brugge. We designed bookcases that can rotate on their axis, a bright-red steel display table, a trapeze-shaped wooden storage volume, an aluminium reception desk and a cruciform table under two copper-scaled fixtures. / 138

/ 139 140 141

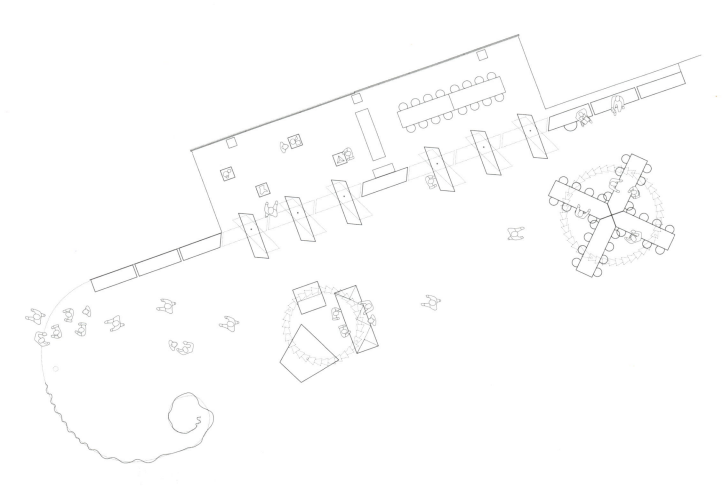

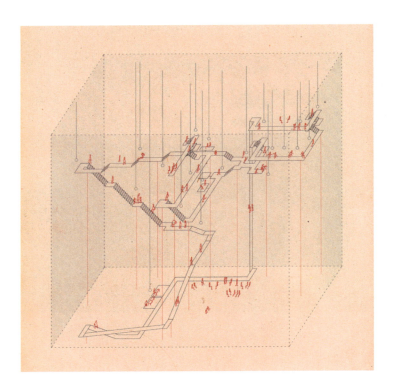

A public route opens up the concert hall and its architecture by Robbrecht en Daem architecten. A trail of wooden spheres guides the public through the spaces. / 142 143 In collaboration with Kabvis

A collection of different mineral spheres refer to the works of art that can be seen relating to the building on the trail. / 144

The spheres cast a soft shadow on the concrete walls. Signage relates to this shadow. / 145

Signage and guiding float through the building.
/ 146 Jan van Eyck, *The Annunciation* (detail), c. 1436 (oil on canvas transferred from panel)

How can a wellness building integrate itself into a landscape? / 147

We first discovered an affinity between the wellness building and a submarine, a compact arrangement of hydraulic components and functions stranded in the landscape. / 148

We then separated the different functions of the programme from each other and granulated the different wellness elements into the landscape and the open air. / 149

The wellness building thus became a scenographic sequence of actions and rituals between indoor and outdoor climates, separate moments in the landscape, with an outdoor room at its centre as a fire room. This instinctive approach starts from the experience of space, from atmosphere, perception and the conscious notion of comfort and discomfort. Inside and outside. / 150

Outdoor classrooms are incorporated into the structure of the school building.
/ 151 J. Duiker and B. Bijvoet, Open-air school, Amsterdam, 1927–30

The concrete skeleton of the school in Waregem was conceived as a stacked ground level. Within that space frame, there are heated and ventilated classrooms. All circulation takes place outdoors, so that students who change room between classes can always get outside for a moment and have a view of the town.
/ 152

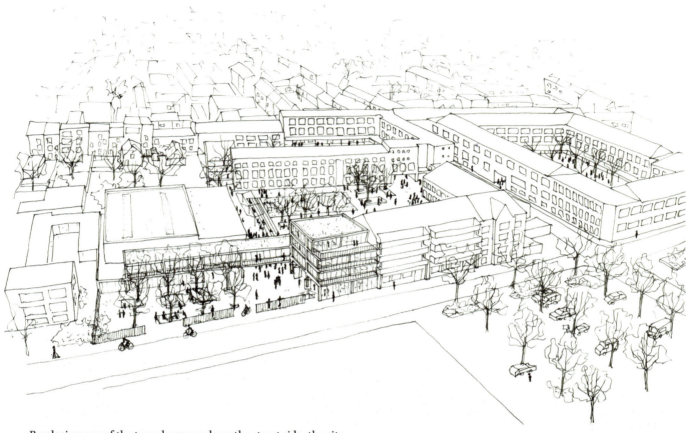

By placing one of the two playgrounds on the street side, the city block itself was opened up. The open relation with the public domain also allows the playground and the volume along it to function autonomously outside school hours. /153

The block has been folded inwards so that the school is no longer a closed bastion, but a function that interacts with the city. /154

For the redesign of the foyer of Concertgebouw Brugge (2017), we created a light fitting as a festive figure. No hard line, but a circle spreading soft, warm light. / 155

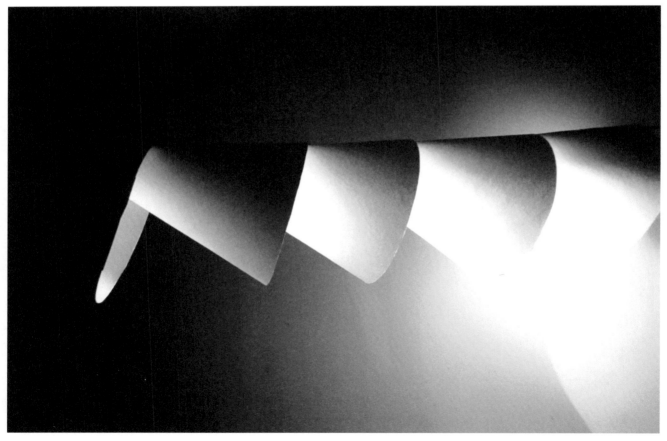

By sliding several folded cones loosely across a light line, we created a sequence of elements that light each other up. The light becomes visible as it shines on the next element. / 156

A flat circle segment in red copper folded into a cone. A simple gesture. The red, untreated copper heightens the light intensity. / 157

A place created by the low-hanging light. A scaly fitting, almost animal-like. / 158

A simple little lamp for a restaurant in Lille (2017). Using a soft clay mould, we made 150 lamps from polyester. Since the clay of the mould is still malleable, each lamp has its own shape. A bit rough, like the dried skin of an animal.

/ 159 In collaboration with Gert Van Dessel

We used the actual hardness and technicity of LED lighting in the design for a nightclub in Lille (2013). Its linear character formed the basis for a pattern that defined the design of the nightclub. The rhythm of the music is captured in the colour and intensity of the pattern.

Set in a black box under a school, the club is an electrifying world where only the light elements and the vibration of the bass tones provide any spatial reference. An ephemeral and illusory space, where you are free to dance and let loose. The repetition of the line pattern expands the space endlessly, making it rarefied and abstract. / 160 161

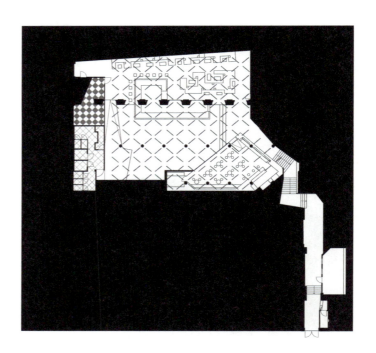

The decorative pattern of the separate smokers' corner, away from the dance floor, was inspired by a camouflage technique used on battleships. / 162

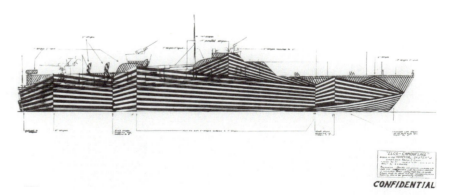

By breaking the shape up into different elements, the ship is no longer recognizable as such. / 163 From: *Deceptively Colorful: US Navy Camouflage during World War II* (2020)

For the house in Halvemaanstraat in Ghent (2003), we made a sheltered, intimate shower stall at the request of the client. Almost womb-like. / 164

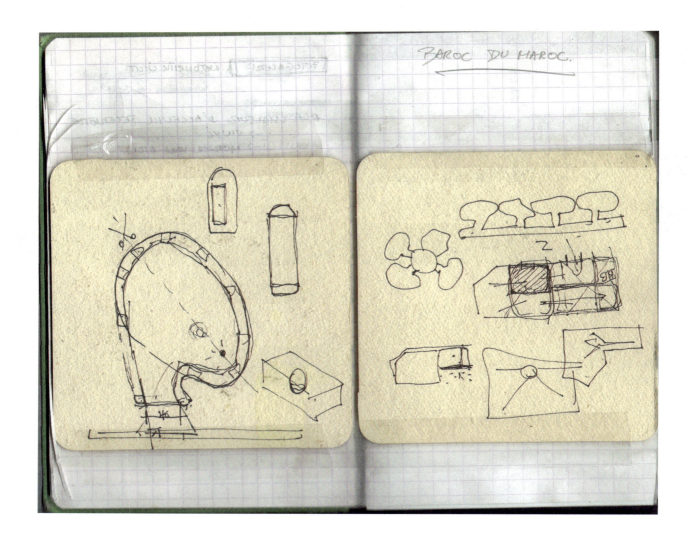

The shower is an ovoid space. When you shower using hot water, there is nothing but a misty, steaming niche. You lose any spatial reference there. / 165 166

A crack in the wall leads to the shower stall. / 167

The small B&B in Lierneux (2015) was developed around the concept of the niche as a compact sheltered space overlooking the surroundings. / 168

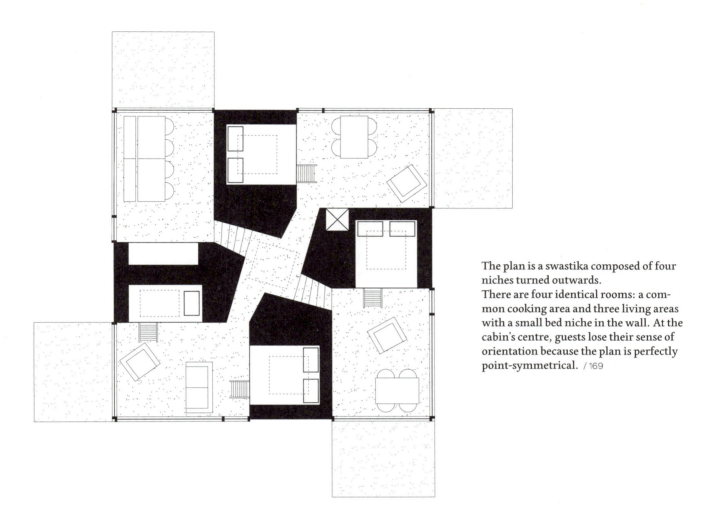

The plan is a swastika composed of four niches turned outwards.
There are four identical rooms: a common cooking area and three living areas with a small bed niche in the wall. At the cabin's centre, guests lose their sense of orientation because the plan is perfectly point-symmetrical. / 169

Once in a room in one of the corners, you can use the view of the surroundings to determine where you are. / 170 171 172

The experience of being forced to spend the night, unprepared, on a ridge, just above the tree line, taught us how to build a primary shelter for yourself. You look for a crevice in a rock, which you first heat by setting fire to brushwood, so that the rock face heats up completely. After removing the ash, you use fresh grass to form a blanket.

/ 173 A shelter prepared by Armand Eeckels in the mountains of Guatemala

The design of the fireplace by Armand Eeckels and Mieke Van der Linden in their own home in Ghent (2014) goes back to that primary experience of seeking warmth and shelter alone and above the ground. Not only does the fire itself provide warmth, but the mass around the fire radiates warmth for a very long time. / 174

The fireplace element consists of 15 cm layers of dry concrete, poured in a fading formwork of fine slats.
Sitting in the niche, you are connected to the fire. It is a cultural interpretation of the lived, physical moment in nature.
/ 175

The combination of dry concrete poured in layers and white concrete poured in horizontal slatted formwork. A mockup to determine the right colour of concrete for the green core. /176

The top two floors of an existing apartment building on the Belgian coast (2016) were demolished and four new storeys were added. /177

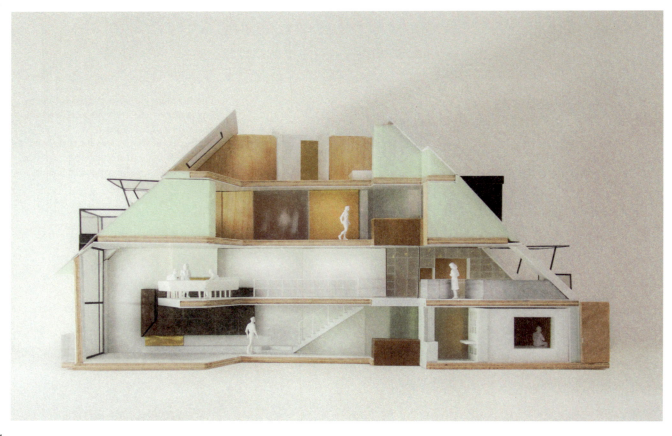

On the 7th, 8th, 9th and 10th floors, we added a solid concrete block with a vertical core. We carved spaces and functions out of the block. / 178 179

The vertical core is composed of 30 cm porous layers of dry concrete. A slow, experimental building method, giving the element a rock-like character. / 180

The formwork of the bathroom cubicle of the flat in Knokke, ready to be filled with white concrete in the workshop.
/ 181 In collaboration with Concreet (Lieven Goetinck en Jeroen D'hondt)

The bathroom cubicle is a coral-like niche. The solid cast and polished sculpture contains a complex programme of techniques, including thermostatic taps, wall heating, drains, rails and controls.
/ 182

The coastal project has a specific terrazzo composed of marble powder and blue glass. The glass pieces are 8 to 10 mm deep, lending depth to the floor and reflecting the light from the sea in a unique way.
/ 183

A rough but bright bunker on the eighth floor. The flat's character lies in the solidity of the walls and floors that give off the diaphanous light. The large guillotine window slides all the way open, allowing the fresh sea air to flow in. Nothing else is needed. / 184

The different types of concrete – now rather rough, now rather refined – capture the bright light in their own unique way. / 185

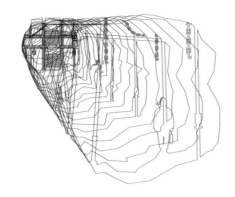
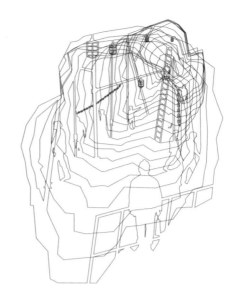
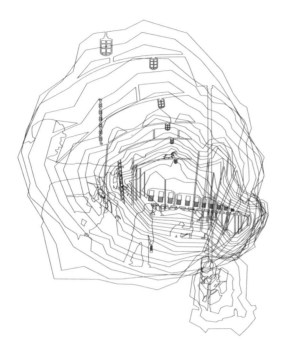

As part of C-mine Expedition in Genk (2012), several installations disclose different aspects of the mining past of this site. Made of thin layers of paper and a moving light, this installation conveys the vastness of the underground tunnels.
/ 186 In collaboration with Kabvis and Create

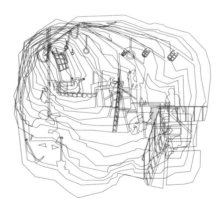
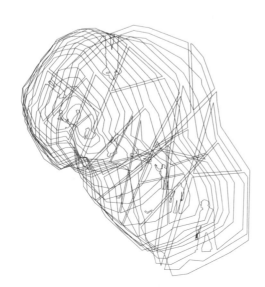
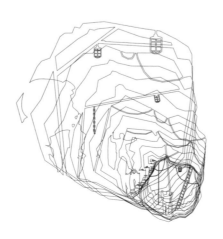

As the light moves slowly through the tunnels, different silhouettes appear and disappear to the rhythm of an audio story. / 187

The translucent bathroom cubicle for the Boxy residence in Sint-Martens-Latem (2006). / 188

The bathroom cubicle was not built, but the specific material research did lead to the production of several translucent honeycomb panels, including some that we still use as worktops in our office today.
/ 189

The intrinsic beauty of nature encountered while ice climbing: a frozen waterfall reveals so many different depths of light and material. Fragile, and yet very strong. / 190

In the early years of our collaboration (2004–06), we did a lot of material experiments with glass-fibre-reinforced materials. We were looking for a strong but thin, translucent sandwich panel. Many materials were tested, from cardboard rolls and textiles to honeycomb structures. / 191

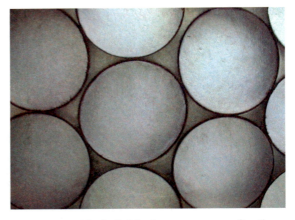

The individual components are fragile and limp, but together they become a rigid composite which light shines through in a unique way. / 192

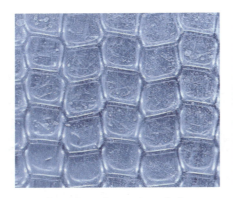

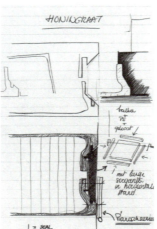

By pushing the polyester into the honeycomb, the edges of the cells pull towards each other through cohesion. This creates a whimsical texture, each cell reflecting light in a different way.
/ 193 194

A cutting instrument using fuse wire to narrow the honeycomb at the edges. The precise execution process was manual and exploratory. / 195

An atelier annex to our office where various honeycomb panels were made in large flat moulds. /196

The translucent material used as a sliding panel in the Boxy pavilion (2009). / 197

The material research also led to the
production of a shadowless table:
Table 01 (2005). / 198

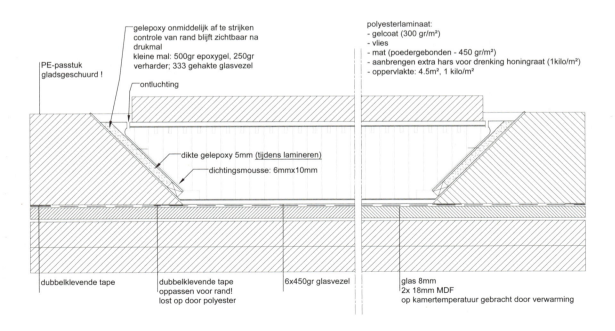

Table 01. / 199

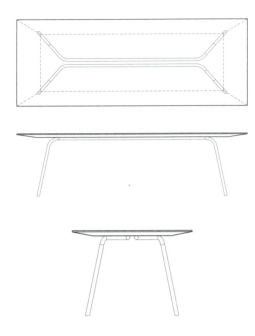

To produce these shadowless tables for the Linq office building in Sint-Denijs-Westrem (2006), we turned our office into a manufacturing workshop. / 200 201

The table possesses the smoothness of a sheet of glass but the warmth of an insulating material. The edges are finished with a crystalline paste that allowed the table to have straight and illuminated edges. / 202

Table 01 (2005) in the Linq office building. / 203 In collaboration with Arunas Arlauskas

For one of our first projects, Linq in Sint-Denijs-Westrem, our ambition was to challenge Mies van der Rohe's Barcelona Pavilion, a symbol of modernism. We started from the structure: two horizontal slabs between which a number of walls were placed and materialized very precisely. / 204

We kept the free plan but added a sculptural roof that draws in light and generates views. This roof shape helped us to achieve a more powerful spatiality.
/ 205

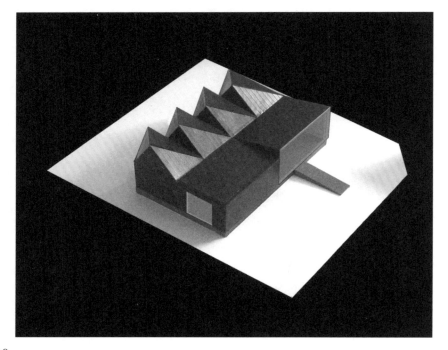

The typology of the shed roof is divided here into four separate domes rotated at 45°. They only let in northern light.
/ 206

Taking the functionality of the plan, the views and the special quality of light as our guidelines, we produced an idiosyncratic building. An object with four different façades, not unlike a UFO that has landed in a typical Flemish allotment. / 207

We owe the sharp lines we had envisaged to a dedicated craftsman who expertly finished off every joint using Swiss techniques. With the precision of a silversmith. / 208 209

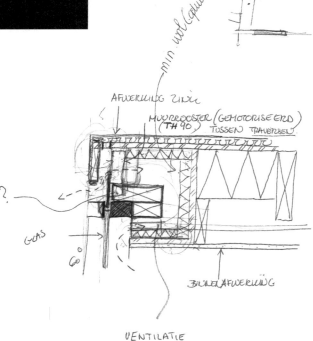

The plan underlying Linq is a swastika. In Hinduism and Jainism, the swastika stands for the life force. At each corner of the house, you get a rotated view and engage in a relation with the surroundings. The sawtooth lines of the concrete slab incorporate the ratio system of the golden section. Walls have been placed on it in a rotating movement from the most public to the most intimate space.
/ 210

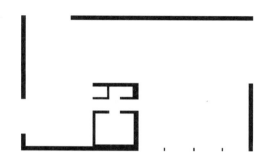

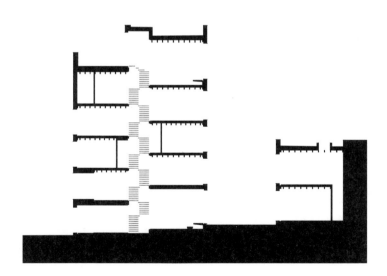

Whereas the development of the Linq project was largely guided by the plan (top), that of the house in Bagattenstraat in Ghent (2019) relied on the cross-section (bottom). / 211

The house stands on a very narrow plot next to the Ghent State Archives by Robbrecht en Daem architecten. / 212

The house was designed according to a system of split-levels. The floors of the front and rear sections each leap half a storey in relation to each other. From the ground level on the street side, you ascend scenically to the studio at the back. / 213

The staircase structure is literally the backbone of the house. The various spaces are attached to it alternately, like leaves on a stem. / 214

A vertical, continuously rising landscape.
/ 215 Charlotte Rudolph, *Mary Wigman's Dancing Hands*, 1928

The house has an inverted layout: the top is home to the living area with roof garden and views over the city while the bottom accommodates the reception and sleeping areas. / 216

The façade material reflects light into the narrow courtyard. The profiled stainless-steel cladding absorbs the light and colours of the surroundings. As a result, the small house integrates wonderfully well into the fabric of the city. / 217

The base is made of robust concrete, shuttered with the same corrugated stainless-steel sheet as the façade above it. From the outside, the house looks like a tin box wrapped around a warm, wooden interior. / 218

The reversal of cool, hard materials and soft, warm materials.

/ 219 Rachel Whiteread, *Vitrine Objects*, 2009

Each staircase generates its own logic in its own context and in doing so it generates a different architecture each time.

The stair as a filter, an obstruction, which at the same time generates interesting views. / 220 House in Bagattenstraat, Ghent, 2019

The staircase to make new connections between different indoor and outdoor spaces. / 221 Tentoonstellingslaan, Ghent, 2012

The staircase as a garden landscape.
/ 222 Haeck house, Sint-Martens-Latem, 2015

The staircase as part of a piece of furniture.
/ 223 House in Bomastraat, Ghent, 2009

The staircase as public space.
/ 224 School campus, Waregem, 2019

The staircase as a catwalk and place to hang out.
/ 225 Bar Mother, Lille, 2013

The staircase in our own office, built with our staff. The staircase as team-building exercise. / 226 NU architectuuratelier office, Ghent, 2020

The staircase as a fine steel structure projecting from a stringer.
/ 227 Haeck house, Sint-Martens-Latem, 2015

The staircase as a spiralling stack of identical blocks in solid wood. / 228 Victoria Theatre, Ghent, 2006

When renovating an existing house in Kessel-Lo, we positioned the staircase as a delicate structure in the window towards the garden. The challenge was to develop a very light staircase that would not obstruct the views onto the garden. Every element of the feather-light steel staircase, including the balustrade, serves a structural function. It was tested in the workshop.
/ 229 230 House Kessel-Lo , 2009

The suspended fyke staircase. / 231 C-mine, Genk, 2012

The staircase expressing a transformation in the public space. The double helix brings visitors from underground in a closed staircase up to 15 m above the public square. An open staircase on top makes the countermovement, spiralling back underground.
/ 232 C-mine, Genk, 2012

Each concrete step is mirrored below and above and rotates around a central reinforcement axis that is tensioned after stacking. / 233

Double steps, ready to be stacked. / 234

Stacking the same element each time with a slight rotation creates a complex geometry. But a child with a crane could actually build this staircase. The model of the staircase is an autonomous representation of the project. / 235

C-mine Expedition in Genk (2012) is an architectural walk that takes you underground, through technical spaces leading to the climb of the shaft tower. Mining infrastructure that was never intended for humans. / 236

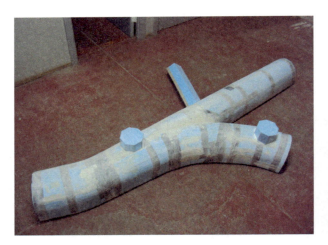

Spatial instruments have been added here and there in the underground ventilation tunnels as cultural inserts. They explain the social and technical history of the mine from a cultural and artistic point of view. / 237 238 Mould of the ventilation tunnels

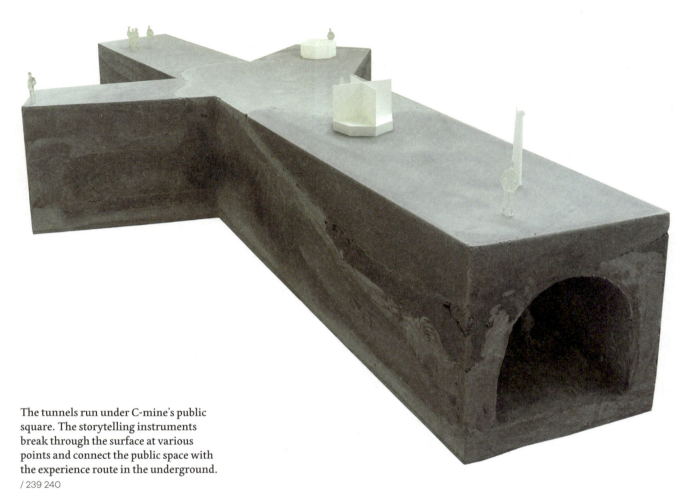

The tunnels run under C-mine's public square. The storytelling instruments break through the surface at various points and connect the public space with the experience route in the underground.
/ 239 240

 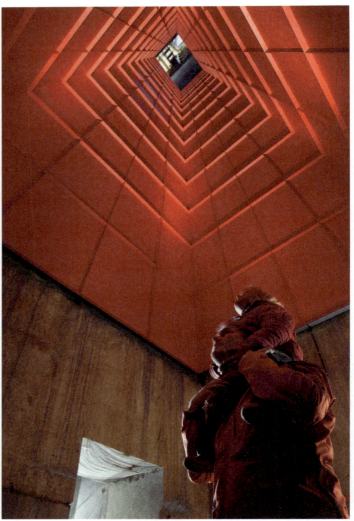

A skylight and periscope, storytelling cones, a sound cell and perspective domes.
/ 241 242

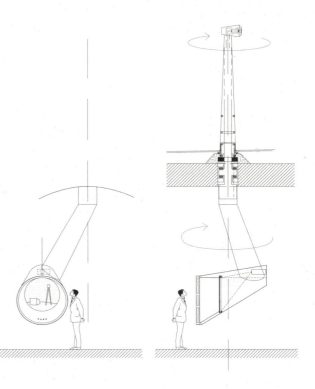

Making the periscope in the workshop. Thorough engineering precedes the seemingly simple shape of the periscope. The robust periscope must be able to rotate through +360° to provide a panoramic view of the upper square. Additionally, turning a large vertical wheel, the periscope takes you back in time and shows you how the landscape changed.
/ 243 244 245

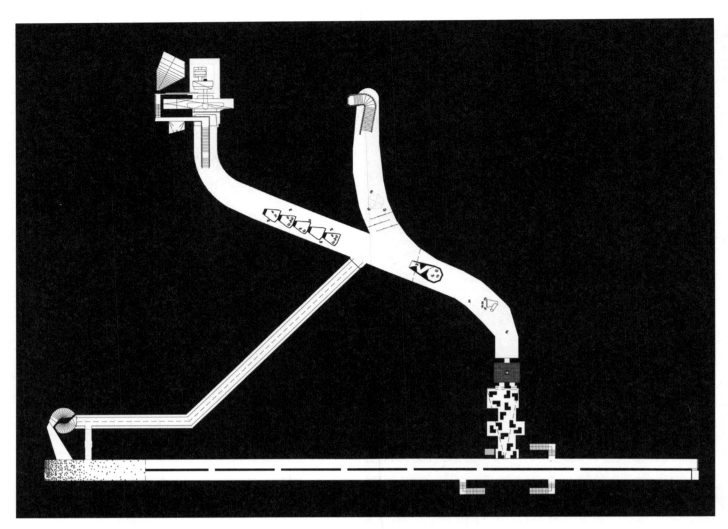

The nice thing about the C-mine project is that there is no reference for it. During the design, you work with matter and space tight around your body. And because everything takes place underground, the space that is made is actually matter we remove. There is no outside, only inside.
/ 246 247

We also applied the idea of building below the Earth's surface in Ordos, a city in a northern province of China, in Inner Mongolia (2008). / 248 Crack in the earth

The new city lies in an area of the Gobi Desert where it gets very hot in summer and freezing cold in winter. A new district with a hundred large villas is being planned in this landscape under the curatorship of Ai Weiwei. / 249

Armand photographing the crater-like spaces in a stretch of eroded desert, the inspiration for our design. / 250

For the *Ordos 100* project, Ai Weiwei and Herzog & de Meuron invited a hundred young international architecture offices to design a villa in a subdivision whose concept and layout were developed by Ai Weiwei. It was intended as a model neighbourhood, a collection of progressive international architecture.

/ 251 photo taken in Ordos, China, 2008

When each firm placed its villa design in the overall model and the district appeared like a lavish buffet of very diverse dishes, an uneasy feeling crept over us. We knew we had made the right choice for ourselves to disappear beneath the Earth's surface. This allowed us to respond appropriately to the context and weather conditions of that place and to preserve some open space in the new district. / 252

Above all, it was an investigation into building below ground and how to establish relationships there between inside and outside and between the spaces themselves. We developed an introvert pentagonal plan in which most of the spaces give out onto an even lower patio. Circulation forms the outer edge of the plan and connects the spaces and views to the patio. / 253 254

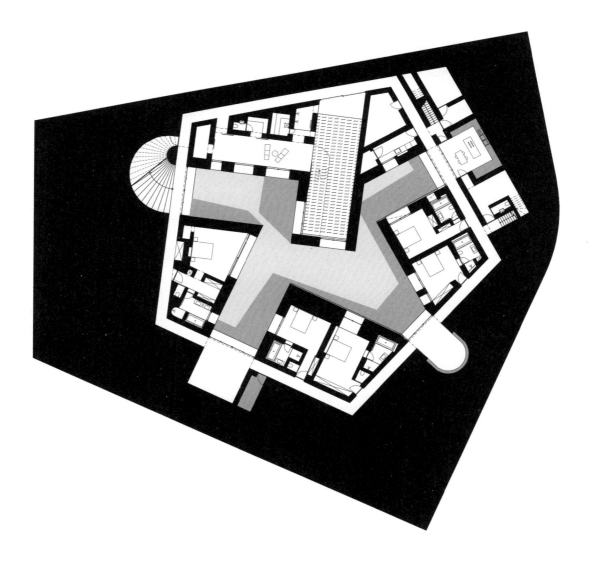

The pentagon as a figure recurs in a number of projects. It is an interesting figure that, with one side more than a square, generates a free dynamic. This house in Landskouter (2014) turns the *Ordos 100* plan inside out. Serving functions are at right angles to more closed sides and the living spaces are turned completely outwards. / 255

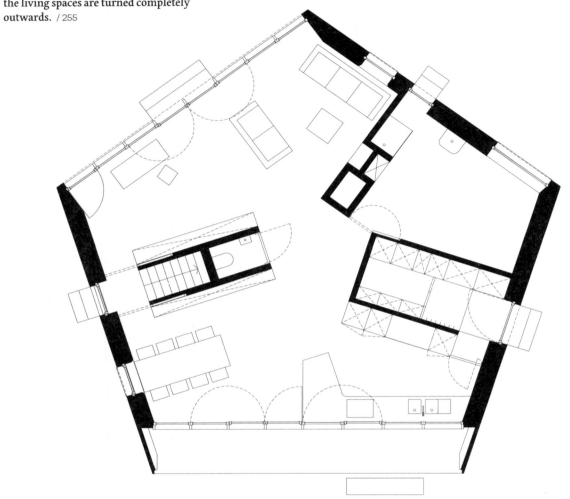

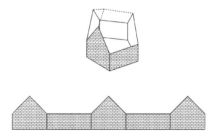

The house replaces a small farmhouse that defied the local planning guidelines. The design translates the typology of consecutive side and end façades that had to be retained. The addition of an extra end wall creates the pentagon. / 256

The result is a highly compact house with façades that differ strongly from each other. Besides a small window and door giving onto the garden, this side façade is completely closed. / 257

By contrast, this end façade is fully glazed. The house is all-sided and has no specific front or back. As a result, all areas of the garden are charged.

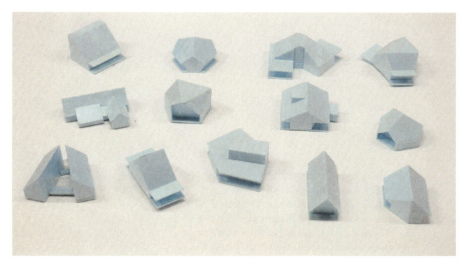

Typological experiments. / 258

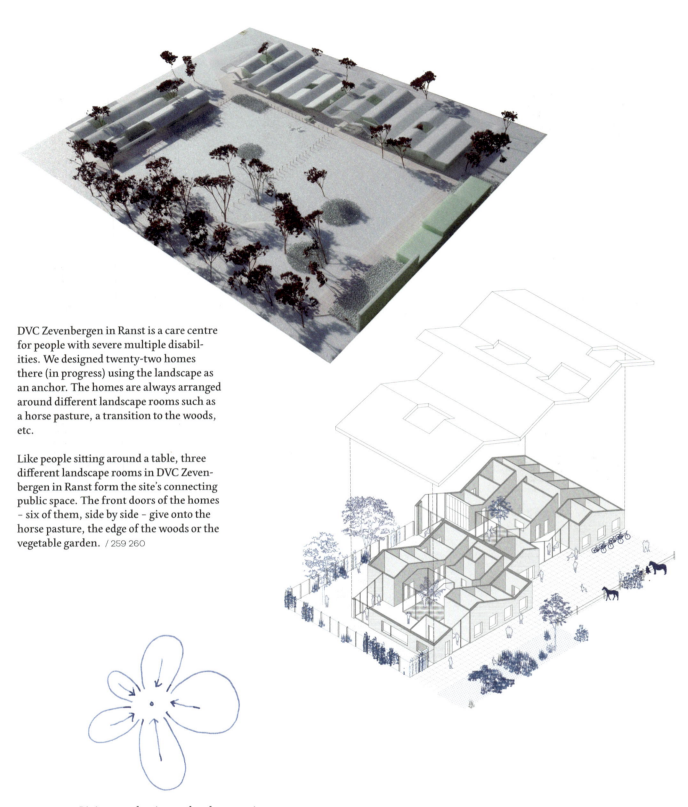

DVC Zevenbergen in Ranst is a care centre for people with severe multiple disabilities. We designed twenty-two homes there (in progress) using the landscape as an anchor. The homes are always arranged around different landscape rooms such as a horse pasture, a transition to the woods, etc.

Like people sitting around a table, three different landscape rooms in DVC Zevenbergen in Ranst form the site's connecting public space. The front doors of the homes – six of them, side by side – give onto the horse pasture, the edge of the woods or the vegetable garden. / 259 260

Living together is a goal and a necessity, but also a possible source of friction and conflict between residents. The living space of the home is designed in such a way that each resident has their own spot from which to connect with the carer who ensures a peaceful and trusting environment. / 261

Just as separate spots in the living area can be closed off, the site as a whole is also closed off. We learned that it is precisely this restriction that gives the residents their freedom. It allows them to move around the site freely. Inclusion nevertheless is an important aspect, even when the spatial setting seems to contradict this quality. It is too difficult for many of the residents to feel safe in the complexity and unpredictability of a city or residential area. Conversely, we can invite that outside world onto the site by, for instance, opening up the petting zoo, integrating allotments with vegetable gardens for the neighbourhood and offering a horseriding trail. / 262 263

For the Emiliani project, a residential facility for residents with mild disabilities, care is integrated as much as possible into the village of Zaffelare. In this way, a rich, open care environment is created in which each resident can take up a personal and meaningful role in society. By letting them lend a hand in the school, for example, or engage in elderly care or help at the bakery around the corner. We learn trough different projects that a form of collective living with a care requirement can be the driving force behind the vibrancy and social cohesion of a neighbourhood. A beautiful interaction and mutual dependency. / 264

There is no fixed typology for care projects. It is important to always recognize yourself, to design spaces where you yourself wanted to live, no matter how specific the care demand may be. / 265

On the wooded part of the site, we arranged the new homes so that a number of trees could be preserved and lived around. Gradual transitions are essential, the spatial stepping stones from public space to private room. Everyone should be able to find their appropriate place with their personality, both resident and neighbour. This is where the connection with the village arises. / 266

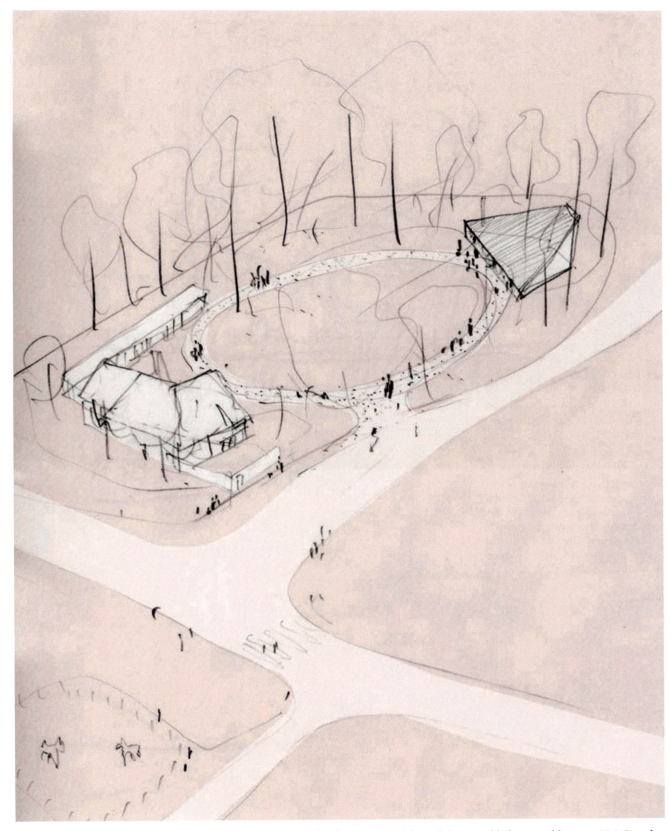

By turning the closed-off garden of the villa into a publicly accessible space, Huis Perrekes engages strongly with the village. Sharing the peace of the lush green oasis. The garden pavilion is an important link in this respect. It is where the choir rehearses and where lectures, concerts and exhibitions are organized. The garden and pavilion are liminal or linking spaces that introduce the outside world to the activities of Huis Perrekes, where people with dementia live. / 267

The roof of the pavilion comes down sharply, generating an intimate indoor space. The façade can slide all the way open, establishing a generous relation with the garden. The pavilion itself can also become the stage, with the audience sitting in the garden. / 268

Whereas the front looks out broadly onto the garden, the back is narrow and high. A high window lets light in from above.
/ 269

The pavilion was conceived as a wooden chest around which a concrete mantle has been cast. The formwork led to a nice graphic and sculptural expression. / 270

Death mask of a house. This porcelain model shows a country house near Ghent. The house was in poor condition, but the owners were attached to its romantic character. / 271

/ 272 *Napoleon I, Emperor of the French,* Death mask, Gipsformerei, Staatliche Museen zu Berlin

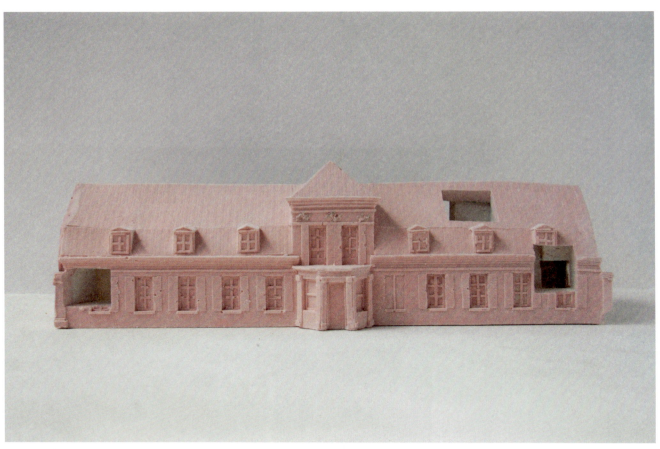

We proposed to make an imprint of the existing house with a full-size mould in which the new house would be cast in a solid concrete shell. In this mask of the original house, the new openings would be cut out according to the new plan structure. / 273

Although this project was ultimately not realized, it turned out to be an interesting conceptual study on the skin as memory, on heritage. / 274

The façade as porous skin. Thanks to its specific texture, the façade becomes receptive to what the atmosphere carries, such as moss, insects, dust, water ...
/ 275 Photo taken somewhere on the road

To finish a small tower in Huis Perrekes, this ancient technique was applied, together with residents and children, using hands and fingers in the soft plaster.
/ 276

This self-made roll with studs served to make the plaster of the tower surface rougher. / 277

The result is a tactile and rough surface on which light materializes the curve. / 278

These large-scale industrial remnants form the rough memory landscape from which we are developing a new public square in Belval, Luxembourg.
/ 279 In collaboration with SNCDA, 2018

The ambition is to make it an open, accessible meeting place. The authentic industrial heritage can give rise to a diversified use and programme, leading spontaneously to a new identity. / 280 281

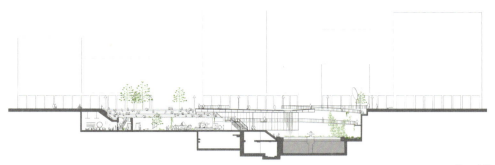

By adding a circular disc as a public space to the two round sunken mineral gardens, this place becomes a connecting space. / 282

The logic of the infrastructure continues in the design: the new disc was conceived as a subtle funnel shape, with one central opening for drainage into the open basin below. / 283

How do we develop a naturally authentic public space? Instead of designing a floating swimming pool in the Vaartkom in Leuven (2020) as requested, we challenged the question with a more ambitious plan: the transformation of a large part of the Vaartkom itself into a swimming zone. The water quality already allows this at many times today. The project becomes a publicly visible barometer for improving water quality. We consider swimming in open water as an evident and natural activity in a city. / 284

How care develops and anchors itself spatially in its context has become an important line of questioning in our work in recent years. In this Pilot Project for Invisible Care developed with Archipelago for the centre of Sint-Truiden (in progress), we allow the care programme to granulate into a mixed-use programme and new urban space: a natural blend of residential and care programme, small ateliers and the possibility of bringing care into different regular housing typologies.
/ 285 286

DING DONG!
"Excuseer, is hier een fietsherstelplek in de buurt?"

"Zullen we even rusten op het bankje daar, opa?"

"Goed geslapen Franky?"
"Neen, ik had het veel te koud deze nacht!"
"Oei, dan zal ik je winterdeken maar uithalen!"
"Heel graag, merci!"

'Het is toch een schoon zicht é, Irma?'

"Rik, breng jij Olivia naar de crèche en dan drinken we nog een koffietje in de brasserie voor ik naar kantoor ga?"
"Nadia, het is zondag! Waar zit jij met je gedachten. Laat die gsm nu eens los en geniet van 't weekend!"

"Zo'n wandelingetje door de bostuin kan toch deugd doen."
"Absoluut, je zou bijna vergeten dat je in de stad bent."

"Echt gezellig om hier koffie te drinken Nadine. Jij hebt het mooiste terras van Sint-Truiden!"

"Prachtig optreden! Fijn dat ik dat nog zo dicht bij huis kan meemaken."

'Care makes city' as the starting point. Workshops for people with disabilities will be provided centrally in the base. There will be a crèche and housing for people with dementia. We develop various spaces that encourage communal use and strengthen the neighbourhood.
A services centre, commercial spaces and regular residential spaces in different typologies intertwine with the surrounding historical urban fabric with small squares and shortcuts across the site. / 287

"Krantje, zonneke, verse fruitsap! Wat moet een mens nog meer hebben?!"

"Verdomde slakken! Sla met gaten, dat wil niemand toch eten!"
"Maar Christine, zie het als een compliment. Die beestjes zijn fan van je kroppen."

"Ik ga bij Wiric nog snel even koekjes halen voor we de kindjes oppikken!"

"LUC, WAAR MAG IK DIE VERSE TOMATEN ZETTEN VOOR DE SOEP?!?"

"Danny, zet jij de stoelen en tafels dan klaar in de kleine polyvalente zaal. Het is weer Bingo-Sunday!"

"Mogen wij nog 2 koffies en 1 stukje vlaai alsjeblieft?"

"Ik had het niet gedacht, maar dit is toch een erg gezellig pleintje geworden!"
"Zie je wel oma, 't was niet allemaal beter in jouw tijd hé."

'Jacqueline, hier schenken ze nu eens de beste koffie uit heel Sint-Truiden.'

Designing a hospital means developing a public space.
We develop the public space as a complement to and in close dialogue with the logistical and medical-technical apparatus. This public space should generate orientation and introduce a human scale to the architecture of hospitals. / 288

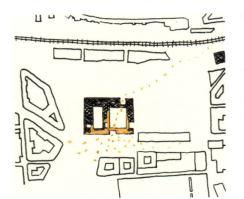

Sketches of four hospitals:

AZJP: at the Cat site in Vilvoorde, there was no prior context we could respond to. The building itself was the first step in the development of a public space.
The hospital generated the public space on the Cat site around it.

Bracops: the public space is externalized and thus strengthens the existing surrounding public space.

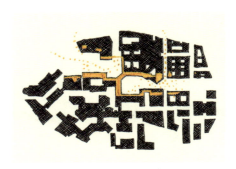

Gasthuisberg: we monitor and develop the public space as an internal body in the campus.

Sint Jan: the hospital here is part of an urban building block, where we let the public space network with the existing public flows.

The renewal of the Bracops Hospital in Anderlecht (in collaboration with Archipelago) can also play its role in the urban fabric, by pushing the public front forward in the new hospital and creating a strong interaction with the surrounding urban space.

/ 289 In collaboration with Archipelago

Study for the façade. / 290 291

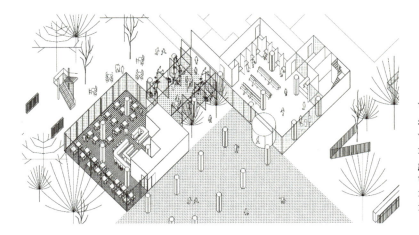

Whereas public circulation is often strongly interiorized in hospitals, here we keep it on the outside, generating a new park space that connects the various green structures in Anderlecht. Beneath the polyclinic, pushed forward, there is room for a restaurant as an autonomous function, aimed at the neighbourhood.

/ 292

Quality indoor spaces are created by engaging them with outdoor spaces and by paying close attention to the boundary between inside and outside. / 293 294

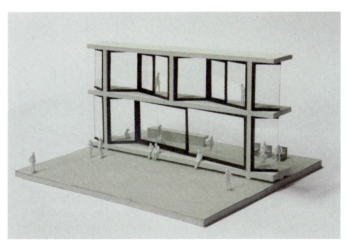

Building components become furniture: places where you can sit, shelter or spend some time. / 295

For Campus Gasthuisberg (Leuven), too, we think parallel to the constant development of the site, about the public dimension of this piece of hospital city conceived as an Italian village on a hill. How do you get around in here? What makes you feel at ease? What develops autonomously and what is the connecting project? / 296 297

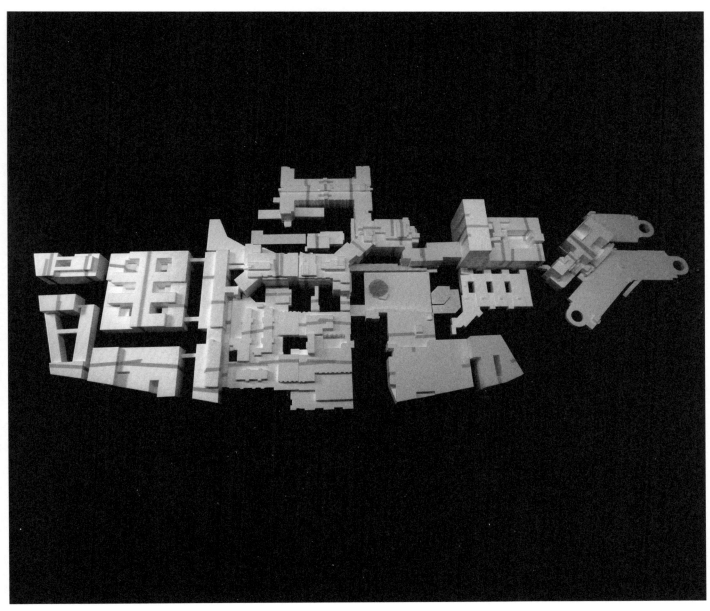

The project for Gasthuisberg involves a recognizable basic circulation, an internal public backbone, developed in parallel with the whole transformation process of this campus.
A palette of indoor and outdoor pieces of furniture, canopies and signage give this public domain an identity. / 298

The benches have a soft pyramidal surface: inside in wood, outside in concrete. There is also a perforated lighter steel variant developed for outdoors. They generate recognizable spots in the hospital's large-scale machinery. / 299

A prototype of the theatrical bench that provides intimacy and orientation in the public space. / 300

The concrete bench put to the test. / 301

A lighter variant of the bench for Gasthuisberg, in perforated steel. / 302

For Bracops, we designed an ergonomic wooden bench that, due to its modular structure, can be applied in different configurations. / 303

A canopy on the scale of the urban outdoor space allows you to get around part of the site of Gasthuisberg without getting wet.
/ 304 305

Wooden 1:1 mock-up of a first variant.
/ 306

Structure is often a game, a trial of strength that leads to legible, elegant solutions. / 307 *Floating roof*, Dobrava, Oton Jugovec / 308

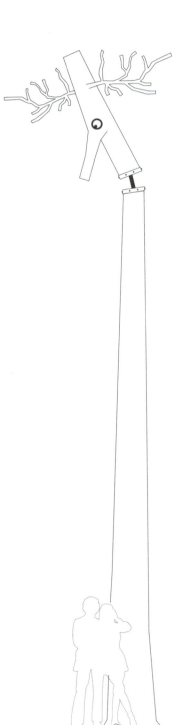

In Kattevennen, at the entrance to the Hoge Kempen National Park, Genk we developed a playful narrative project in collaboration with Mathilde Geens (Kabvis).
The Stokkeman (Stickman)route (2021) is a walk along these imaginary forest dwellers.
/ 309 310 311

Making a stickman like a child, but on a much larger scale. Inspiration for the Stickmen is to be found in the trees themselves. Flip a branch, give it eyes and you get a figure that speaks to the imagination. Each Stickman has its own story and has something to say in a humorous and poetic way about the fragility of their habitat, aspects of sustainability, what a forest means, what our planet means in relation to the universe, and so on. / 312

Giganticus sleeps. / 313

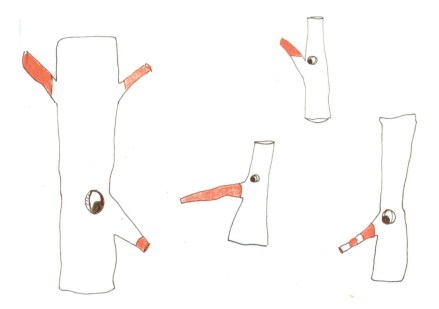

This picture shows a biologist searching frantically for a specific plant. This is not unlike the way we make architecture. With the full commitment of our team, we have embarked on a journey of discovery that takes us to unexpected places. We gradually discover new roads, each new road exerting its own influence on us.

NU has steadily grown into the fine group of people with who we now set our course. We consciously try to keep moving and to think about what we are doing, what we would like to do and in what way we can best answer the ambition that unites us.

It is an adventurous journey.

/ 314 *The Plant Hunter Louis Van Houtte*
© FPS Science Policy, on permanent loan to Meise Botanic Garden.

157

Will it be very light or will it be very heavy?

Stefan Devoldere

Architecture Is Making

In the opening chapter of his *Essai sur l'architecture*, Marc-Antoine Laugier describes the genesis of architecture. A primitive man, guided by his instincts, sets out in search of a place to rest. He lies down on the grass beside a stream to enjoy what nature has to offer him. But the sun is shining hard so he seeks shelter in the shady forest. When heavy rain comes down on him through the foliage, a cave offers solace. But it is dark and dank there. So the man builds his own shelter. Using broken branches and fallen leaves, he puts up a primitive hut: 'Thus, man is housed.'[1] Behold, architecture! Or, as Laugier concludes: 'All the splendours of architecture ever conceived have been modelled on the little rustic hut I have just described. It is by approaching the simplicity of this first model that fundamental mistakes are avoided and true perfection is achieved.'[2] The hut helps to distinguish that which is indispensable from whimsy. After all, real beauty lies in necessity.

After his studies, Armand Eeckels spent several months travelling around South America on his own. With no one to count on but himself, he once had to improvise a place to spend the night on a ridge just above the tree line in Guatemala. After finding a crevice big enough, he filled it with brushwood, set fire to it and subsequently added a layer of freshly plucked grass. Like a warm blanket, the radiant heat of the granite helped to get him through the night. The physical experience of that night underpins a fireplace Armand built years later with Mieke van der Linden in his own home. The moment inspired a making process they readily threw themselves into, without quite considering the energy it would require. Carefully poured in gently sloping 15 cm layers, a stylized rock emerged around the fireplace in the living room after six months. This is architecture you can crawl into, architecture that invites physical contact and offers comfort. A niche that cherishes as much as it is cherished.

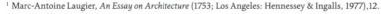

The story of the rock says a lot about the way NU architectuuratelier sees the craft. The eagerly embraced risk, the craftsperson's inventiveness, the matter-of-fact, step-by-step plan, the focus of the moment ... It's not just the end result that matters, the process is essential too. The architects like to compare this to climbing a mountain. An ascent where every moment demands full attention and every detail is essential. And with a clear goal in mind: not the creation of an image, but the shaping of a feeling. A much-used guide in this respect is Bernard Rudofsky's *Architecture Without Architects*, an anthology of vernacular structures that in 1964 sought to deconstruct the myth

---

[1] Marc-Antoine Laugier, *An Essay on Architecture* (1753; Los Angeles: Hennessey & Ingalls, 1977), 12.
[2] Laugier, *An Essay*, 12.

of modern architecture.³ In the absence of a distinct architectural frame of reference, one's own experience is the main guiding principle. Constantly testing and challenging forms and materials, thinking in all sorts of ways with one's hands. The architecture of Armand Eeckels and Halewijn Lievens exists in the present⁴, without concessions and without context.

And yet one of the office's key projects is literally encompassed in a clearly modern architectural oeuvre. For the extension of Sint-Lucas in Ghent, architect Xaveer De Geyter called on the young NU to provide a blind concrete street façade with quirky translucent viewing holes. They came up with the rather ambitious plan to make six transparent plastic blocks to be mounted in the formwork of the concrete wall to be poured on site. The blocks are 35 cm thick and up to 2.5 m long. They each have a meandering outline, different on the inside and outside. Meticulously cut foam forms were used to make a silicone mould into which 1 cm of epoxy resin free of air bubbles was poured daily. Each production step was carefully thought out and tested for effects on hardness, strain and transparency. The tight budget left no room for second thoughts. These are windows without parallel, transparent bricks carved with fuse wire by the pioneers of architecture.

Materiality and Experimentation

NU's architects became fascinated with the making process in Maarten Van Severen's studio, where everything that is conceived can immediately be tested using the necessary tools. They therefore put that making process centre stage when, in 2006, they were invited by the Flanders Architecture Institute and the arts campus De Singel to take part in the *35m³ young architecture* exhibition series, for which a new generation of architects were asked to fill a 35 m³ volume with their emerging design practice. NU loaded the space with the formwork – oiled up and ready for pouring – of the kitchen unit from their first renovation in Halvemaanstraat in Ghent. The silhouette of the unit in the making was drawn in chalk on the outside of the volume. The installation tried to capture the moment of making-together as the engine of their design practice: the office closing for a week so that they can camp out at the construction site, the formwork being hammered together during the first three days; the reinforcement made on the fourth; and the concrete poured and polished on the fifth. Behold, architecture!

The desire to make something with their own hands lingers in every project, but the urge to experiment sometimes threatens to derail them. When adding a new penthouse apartment to a block of flats on the seafront in Knokke-Heist, they pulled out all the stops to push materials and light incidence to the limit. A four-storey light-green concrete circulation core was poured on the seventh floor, from which a number of floor slabs and elegant prefabricated volumes were suspended – for instance, a coral-like bathroom. A large guillotine window provides abundant light that systematically reflects differently on the various

---

³ Bernard Rudofsky, *Architecture Without Architects: A Short Introduction to Non-pedigreed Architecture* (New York: The Museum of Modern Art, 1964).
⁴ 'Nu' is Dutch for 'now'.

finishes and refined compositions of the concrete, including a terrazzo with blue glass shards. Putting an unruly bunker on top of the Atlantic Wall[5] proved to be a challenging balancing act that, in its scale and ambition, stretched the limits of the construction process to the extreme. Likewise, a commission for a translucent bathroom volume in the Boxy house – converted by Maarten Van Severen – had suffered a few years earlier from rising production costs, eventually foundering halfway through. The wall panels already produced were recovered as worktops for their own office space, ultimately evolving into a table for a new project.

The bathroom wall became a 'shadowless table', constructed with a translucent polyethylene honeycomb structure between two layers of polyester laminate. Timing and additives were experimented with to make the table as transparent as possible through slow hardening. Six copies of the table were ultimately made. To this end, a dust-free production line was set up in their own studio. It proved difficult to industrialize, however, due to the extreme error-prone nature of the artisanal manufacturing process. Four of these tables found a home in Linq, the house/office designed with Arunas Arlauskas, a comrade from the early days, and assembled almost as meticulously as the experimental furniture pieces. It is an office masquerading as a house – which it has since become – in a high-profile location in a typical suburban subdivision near Ghent. An environment the building alludes to formally, but which it explicitly rebels against by enveloping itself in black zinc cladding.

The contractor here appears to have been cut from a different cloth than in Knokke-Heist, helping the architects to achieve the high level of finishing (a matter of millimetres rather than the usual centimetres). This resulted in a building with a playful formality that is refined in every detail. Again, light incidence and materialization were given a prominent role. In the corner of each side, a large window catches the view onto and from the surroundings in a way that is constantly changing. Inside, four sculptural skylights define four workplaces in an open plan. The house/office rests on a concrete base, slightly raised above ground level, and stands out as a quirky object in the area. On the corner of a banal commuter road, the product developers have built an architectural lookout that really wants to be looked at. With somewhat arrogant swagger, the house is a literal showcase of exceptional craftsmanship.

A Collection of Actions

It is no coincidence that NU's primitive hut is a kitchen. For their first conversion in Halvemaanstraat, Armand and Halewijn drew up a 'plan of intentions', a sheet of tracing paper that is placed over the existing house and that gives, in concise descriptions, possible interventions and qualities a place in the space. Into that cloud of words, a robust kitchen unit has been inserted, lending a new dynamic to the plan through its mass. The concrete unit collects the essence of cooking, like a ritual turned to stone. A worktop with sink and gas burners is counterbalanced by two benches and a

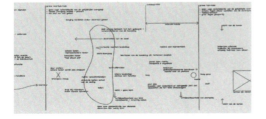

---

[5] The 'Atlantic Wall' is the name given to the uninterrupted line of apartment blocks at the Flemish coast. The term refers originally to the system of coastal defences built by Nazi Germany during World War II.

tabletop. The unit establishes cooking as the centre of the home – it stands even somewhat in the way – and thus radically defines the rhythm of living together. For NU, the place where people cook and eat together is the starting point of any floor plan. The focal point around which life is organized and from which it spreads out into the rest of the home.

So when NU was commissioned by Flemish Government Architect Peter Swinnen to design a workshop, the Atelier Bouwmeester, in the Ravenstein Gallery in Brussels, a kitchen was a *sine qua non*. The Ravenstein Gallery is a covered passage connecting Brussels Central Station with the Centre for Fine Arts further uptown. The shopping gallery dives directly into the train and metro station, at one end, and finishes in a majestic rotunda at the other. The rotunda is circled on either side by staircases leading uptown. On the rotunda's mezzanine, the Team Flemish Government Architect has been given a public workspace behind large glass walls that allow commuters and passers-by to look in. The slightly curved space is at once furnished and structured by a number of striking furniture units. They are all meticulously designed and manufactured objects. Once placed in the space, they develop their own 'force field', with which they influence that space and each other.

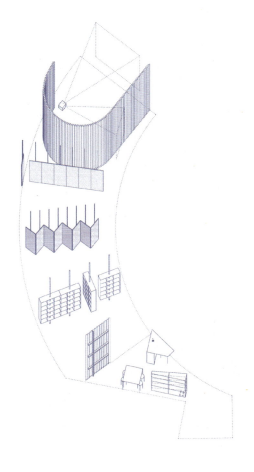

Up against the last window in the row is an aluminium kitchen worktop on a fridge-wide plinth. On the wall behind it hangs an open deep-blue kitchen cabinet. An oversized screen in corrugated polyester separates the kitchen acoustically but lets light through. Four steel bookshelves rotate on their axis and line up neatly with each other. Suspended from the ceiling, mobile presentation boards ensure the flexible layout of the space. A small auditorium is demarcated by a curved double-layer curtain. The various pieces of furniture possess a strong personality, determined by the logic of the uses to which they can be put and the designerly solution applied. At the same time, they refer to the various actions specific to a government architect: a well-stocked library as a source of insights, a kitchen table where compelling conversations take place, an inspiring work session with drawings on tables and walls, a closed jury of the Open Call ... Together, they guide the team's interaction with the outside world and provide the Atelier Bouwmeester with a clear programme, without wanting to define the space itself too strongly.

A similar interplay is at work in the redesign of Concertgebouw Brugge as an 'open house', in collaboration with graphic designer Mathilde Geens. The spacious entrance hall is at once filled in and scaled by various geometric elements. A wall of pivoting bookcases that double as seating areas screens off a small exhibition space in the former cloakroom and forms the backdrop to a counter placed centrally in the space. The location of the counter is marked by a large circular light fitting on which a string of copper lampshades have been slid on their sides. A little further on, a similar majestic chandelier hangs above a large cruciform table which visitors can sit at. A breadcrumb trail of hanging spheres, each with a distinct material character, then draws visitors further into the building for an exploration of the architecture itself and the art it houses.

Community and Shelter

The concrete kitchen island, the steel library, the copper chandelier ... They not only bring to mind Laugier's words, they are also related to the circular tubular piece of furniture that Aldo and Hannie van Eyck placed around the stove in their own living room, like a circle around a campfire. A bench lay on the circle that could be moved closer to or back from the fire as needed. For NU, this piece of furniture illustrates the importance of a reduced design that focuses on use. The playing field of an object in the space appears with an obvious utility that generates its own aesthetic power. A variant of the bench stands in the garden of Huis Perrekes. There, the circle opens up, is duplicated, and two long wooden planks are slid between the frame. The circle defines, literally and figuratively, a place of togetherness.

Huis Perrekes provides assisted living for people with dementia, with a strong emphasis on local embeddedness and keeping things on a small scale. The residential houses, which can accommodate fifteen residents each, are located in an ordinary street in an ordinary village. When a stately doctor's villa with a spacious garden was acquired in Oosterlo, NU was called in to give shape to an exceptional care community. The villa became home to three guest rooms for family, study visits or artistic residencies. There are also two small flats for assisted living. A ground-level extension houses ten rooms for short-term stays and there is additional space for physiotherapy, music therapy and meetings. The typology of the existing doctor's house was taken up as an occasion to experiment with other forms of living and to enrich community life.

The starting point is a familiar, high-quality living environment, with all the activities that go with it. A new kitchen was added at a strategic location. It generously opens onto the living area and the kitchen garden. Everyday rituals give people with dementia something to hold onto, in both space and time. In today's care landscape, they usually disappear from sight for reasons of efficiency (for instance, by being centralized in an industrial kitchen). But here, cooking together makes up the heart of the day. NU designed several focal points for these rituals: the bench in the garden, for instance, and the elegant round table in the living space, furnished with a still life cast in plaster that holds the sectors of the table together. These are objects that deliberately draw residents out of their isolation, even as the time to take one's leave approaches steadily.

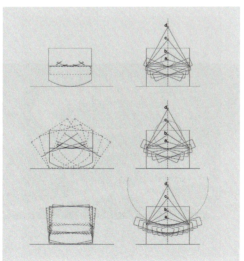

Cradling is the comforting act par excellence, an act that makes maintaining contact with a carer or family member possible until the end. For Huis Perrekes, NU translated that human interaction into a soberly designed cradle bed. It was tested extensively with the home's residents in order to achieve the right radius of curvature for the gentlest rhythm. Geometry in movement, in beauty and safety. The need for social contact is woven into the design of Huis Perrekes on all scales. The showpiece of this new house is the large garden that opens up to the neighbourhood. A pavilion with grand piano confirms the public status of the garden and is the setting for concerts, exhibitions and other events. The pavilion stands tall and narrow among the trees at the rear, growing low and wide towards the garden. A glazed wall slides all the way open. The garden is the window to the world that every house needs. It has also given the village a new momentum, culminating in an annual spring festival.

NU pursues this focus on that village feel in Zaffelare too, where the designers were faced with a remarkable case of déjà vu by the non-profit association Emiliani. A doctor's villa with adjoining park was to provide space for twenty-eight adults with mental disabilities. Here too, the valuable garden was drawn into the house. The villa was extended in the front garden, taking a large chunk of the programme out of the back garden and bringing living closer to the street. This left space at the back for the existing trees, around which a new residential volume was folded along a side street. The strict logic of the care facility is breached with space for spontaneous encounters: in the communal kitchen, in a shared winter garden, in the collectively accessible greenery that interweaves with the residential groups and is cherished as the true attraction of the project.

The Village and the Street

The intention to link meeting spaces to the public domain and deliberately make room for them within the medical apparatus is scaled up in the various hospital designs which NU has been involved in. In Anderlecht, the designers worked hard with Archipelago to puzzle out the interface between the Joseph Bracops hospital and the city. The central circulation route of the healthcare complex was given a transparent face towards the surrounding residential fabric and an externally operated restaurant was inserted under the new polyclinic. The Gasthuisberg university hospital is, of course, a town in itself – or rather, a ski village which, pressed between the Leuven city ring road and the E314 motorway, is in constant danger of falling victim to its own urge for expansion. Like most ski villages, the hospital site also lacked a clear identity. NU was asked to bolster the site's public character by giving shape to everything the visitor comes into contact with.

They did so by designing a public guiding thread that folds itself between and through the amalgam of extensions, both inside and outside the buildings. Plazas, roof gardens, covered promenades, waiting areas and benches are linked together in a formal language that transcends the prevailing chaos of constant change. Gently undulating benches in wood or concrete resonate with the rising and falling articulation of a pleated canopy. Tactile experience and structural logic are the occasion for graceful visual expression and a powerful public gesture. The same goes for Ranst, but then with greater composure. Here, a services centre for people with severe mental disabilities has been radically opened up using the rural village as a model. Between forest and subdivision, NU designed three landscape rooms, each with its own experiential value: allotments, an orchard and a horse pasture. Together they form the yard of a farm, a new central place, with an elongated fallow pasture to connect with the neighbourhood.

The landscape rooms are bordered by various residential houses that are connected by a covered gallery. The houses accommodate eight residents each whose rooms are arranged around a shared living space with patio, as a base for the carer who brings tranquillity to the home. Despite this central point of attention, the plan is also directed fully towards the outside as a place of experience. The rooms have their own or a shared garden, and under the spacious projection of the gallery, the living space is given a considerable extension in the open air. Under the folding roof (here and there in openwork), a diverse spatiality is created both inside the houses and outside at the front door. The porch and yard are given a central role in Ranst as a collective place of significance, both on the scale of the living group and on the scale of the care institution as a whole.

This is already apparent from the cover image of the competition file for the Open Call. A cross-section model shows how the living environment of care residents stretches between the patio of their own home and the public footpath by the horse pasture. The image illustrates how the indoor and outdoor spaces coincide in perfect symmetry in the design, the door to the house acting as a pivotal point. Moreover, it shows sharply how a street, whether covered or not, can enhance a design, but also how a well-designed interior can generate public space. This also emerges in the model of De Centers, the fifty-nine largely unused spaces under the railway arches in Borgerhout, which were made available to local entrepreneurs at the initiative of AG Vespa. On the borderline between inside and outside, NU placed a structure that makes the place both usable and experienceable, and which then opens up in both directions.

On the inside, the Centers have been given a basic layout with a functional mezzanine. On the outside, a steel frame has been placed against the brick arches, projecting a metre from the façade. Some frames are glazed, others open; some are interconnected, others not. This creates different floor areas and usage possibilities. The intervention not only generates space under the tracks, it also creates space just outside the door. With a strong identity and the appropriate transparency, the steel structure subtly mediates between the monumentality of the railway infrastructure and the scale of the pavement and that of a workspace suited for a woodworker, ceramics studio, craft beer brewer. The blind rear of the district thus becomes a lively street where people can shelter, sit down and enjoy some variety. It not only shifts the boundary between the Centers and the area, it also breathes new life into the relationship between the city centre and the fringes.

Between Inside and Outside

This deliberate pursuit of interaction with the street, with public space as a shared place, already appears in one of NU's first projects, the threshold or bench with in-built step created for Xi in Ghent. This coffee house connects two streets and is set back a little from the building line on both sides. This draws the public domain in a little, creating an intermediate space rich in potential. The same goes – but on a larger scale – for the conversion of a former joiner's atelier on Bomastraat. The threshold here becomes a veritable courtyard where workshops and other public events are held under the old shed roof behind the street façade. The building – a five-metre-deep strip across the entire width of the plot – is pushed back, separating the publicly accessible courtyard from the walled-off private garden. In the rear corner of the garden, a work studio has been set up with a terrace sheltered by a remnant of the shed roof.

Frameless windows and wall surfaces that open out engage in a game of visibility and continuity throughout the house, garden and courtyard. When entering from the street, a curved kitchen unit – poured on site by Armand and Halewijn – is partly hidden from view behind an old olive tree. On the other side of the living space, a large bookcase leads to the upper floor, the steps fitted with hardened inlays to protect against wear and tear. At the front, three shipping containers mediate between the house and the city. The first stands crosswise in the courtyard and forms the entry to the dwelling. The other two are stacked on top of the entrance gate and set up as a guest room. Like a periscope, they make living – and the guest bed behind a high window – visible in the streetscape, but just as spectacularly draw the urban landscape into the domestic environment.

A similar movement underlies the plan for the Heilig Hart college in Waregem. Rather than finishing off the street façade with a new wing of classrooms, the extension is folded inwards so as to give space to the town. The new playground becomes a forecourt to the school and literally gives shape to the concept of a 'brede' or 'broad' school (i.e. a community school). The layout of the courtyard and the connection with a ground-level dance hall make possible various scenarios for external use. Everything thus becomes a potential intermediate space. The two new buildings that frame the forecourt consist of a prefabricated concrete structure which the classrooms have been inserted into as air-conditioned boxes. With a clear nod to Jan Duiker's open-air school, all circulation is suspended against and between the structure. The life of the school is thus drawn out onto the galleries and staircases. The pupils are the building. They bring life to the walls of the schoolyard and feed the spectacle of the city.

The same thing happens in Kessel-Lo, where a small apartment building was converted into a spacious single-family house. The façade plane on the garden side has been loaded with a playful dialogue between inside and outside. In the double-height living area, the interior staircase leading to the mezzanine ends up unexpectedly in the window, creating a special place between house and garden: a thickened window frame that has been pushed out of the rear façade into the garden. The oversized concrete windowsill catches the warmth of the sun and invites the occupants to linger, like Armand and Mieke's fireplace or the threshold of the coffee house. The first steps of the stairs have been carved into the concrete, setting the stage for a fine steel structure that climbs up along the window. On the garden side, a pink stepping stone corrects the difference in height. The window becomes an alcove, a space to fully engage in the experience of living. Sitting on a threshold, walking in the façade plane, lazing away in a window: architecture is a distinctly physical experience for NU.

Living in and around a Staircase

In NU's projects, the staircase is repeatedly given a unique architectural elaboration. As a bookcase in Bomastraat, as a stack of building blocks of solid wood in Theaterhuis Victoria, as a slowly ascending flight of steps/garden in the Haeck residence, as an unusual team-building moment with staff in their own office.
The staircase is the architectural element par excellence where the tactile experience of a well-designed object translates into an exceptional spatial experience. On the staircase you walk on and in the architecture, a physical experience that NU invariably charges with constructive challenges and keen technical insight. This is certainly true in the slender house in Bagattenstraat, which, on a plot barely 4 m wide, sits wedged into a blind corner of the Ghent State Archives building. The house's backbone is formed by a six-storey hardwood staircase, which the house climbs up around, one split-level at a time.

On the ground floor, the open staircase structure filters the view onto a reception area that connects to a patio and a back house that serves as a quiet workspace. A little higher, the posts frame an interior view from the shower behind embossed glass. A little higher still, the posts demarcate a breakfast nook in the kitchen. The uninterrupted posts of the staircase are alternately left open, filled in with glass, or form part of a room wall. Structural nodes have been elaborated with care and without unnecessary fuss, concrete floor slabs neatly inserted between the stair sections. Hidden behind the street façade is a lift that pushes the house a bit deeper into the plot. Below the roof terrace, a window in the side façade lets the afternoon sun into the kitchen. The initially introverted character of the house gradually transforms into a light-filled living environment rich in views, with the stylish staircase as its helix and a magnificent cityscape as the cherry on the cake.

Views onto the surrounding landscape also guided the design of a single-family house in Landskouter. In one of the last offshoots of a village ribbon development, NU replaced an old farmhouse with a new variant fitted with an additional gable wall. By adding a gable plane to the archetypal composition, a pentagonal ground plan is created that opens up the house to the rural surroundings. Circulation disappears into three blocks that divide the ground plan like thickened walls. They are each perpendicular to an external façade and connect to a front, side and back door. The two remaining façades are fully glazed and offer views from the house to the front and back. The window plane is set back here in relation to the overhanging roof, which is draped over the remarkable volume like a dark cloak. The house obstinately defies the local planning guidelines[6], but at least its conscience is clear. Bio-ecological materials form a breathable, humidity-regulating ensemble. The house is black, different and distinctly contemporary, but it enters into a sustainable alliance with the greenery in its plan design and technical elaboration.

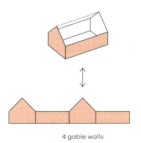

4 gable walls

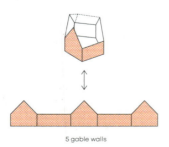

5 gable walls

---

[6] The house is not in a residential zone. It is 'zonevreemd', a planning term which translates literally as 'foreign to the zone', and therefore could not be built as a new house per se. However, as an existing farmhouse it is tolerated as a habitation, planning regulations stating that such farms can be rebuilt if certain rules are followed concerning volume and appearance.

The plan recalls the proposal NU developed in 2008 for ORDOS 100, a project for which Chinese artist Ai Weiwei invited a hundred promising architecture firms worldwide to design a luxury villa in the Ordos Desert in Mongolia. The promotional stunt yielded a throng of flashy architectural demonstrations, which NU deftly evaded by burying itself. An ode to the barren desert landscape waiting to be colonized, the house disappears completely underground. The pentagonal floor plan folds back on living itself. It is arranged around a central outdoor space and girded by an unending circulation, like a radical reversal of Landskouter. A hole in the ground provides shelter under the open sky, keeping the ninety-nine other luxury villas out of sight, and thus safeguarding the image of the unspoilt desert plain. By going underground, NU gives the landscape free rein.

Experience and Landscape

Landscape and underground are connected intensely at the C-mine cultural site in Genk. C-mine Expedition is an experience route in the 5 m wide ventilation shafts of the old Winterslag mining site, supplemented by an underground passage to the head frame and the panorama that goes with it. NU not only provided the architecture, but also curated the content of the route in collaboration with Mathilde Geens. Together with writers, photographers and other artists, they produced, not a scenery that has long vanished, but an architectural experience that links the underground to the vast landscape of the mine development and the many layers of meaning it is made up of. Visitors wriggle between concrete constrictions, wander through a forest of buttressing props, and listen to casual conversations between miners in seemingly endless corridors. Suspended diving bells reveal some arresting mining stories. An oversized periscope looks both up and back into the past. The 884 m deep mine shaft becomes an echo chamber.

The underground route plays on the intuitive experience of space and the feelings that arise in the process – today and in the past. However, the high point of the tour reveals itself at a height of 15 m, from where visitors can enjoy a spectacular vista of slag heaps near and far after rising from the buttressed space through an enclosed staircase. This staircase is constructed as a double helix, fixed with a solid tensile reinforcement in the centre, around which a diameter-wide concrete stair tread rotates step by step. While the descending staircase is open, the ascending one, being closed off from the outside world, builds up to the surprise of the vista. From the intermediate platform, you ascend further to the top of the head frame via a second spiral staircase suspended between the tripod of the head frame. In the step-by-step ascent of the frame, technical bravura and rapture intertwine to produce a unique experience. The showpiece of the mining infrastructure gets a bold contemporary addition.

In Meise too, an extraordinary showpiece was set up as part of the public route through the treasures of the Meise Botanic Garden. Together with Archipelago, NU tackled the overall structure of the park and several buildings in need of renovation. In a brand-new home for the living collection, an ingenious viewing box has been

placed in the middle of several square metres of greenhouse, immersing visitors in the rich plant collection of the Flemish research institute. Visitors embark on an expedition among the tropical plants, a journey of discovery that is masterfully staged from the very first steps towards the greenhouse complex, half concealed between tall greenery. A narrow path leads between high greenhouse walls to a concrete staircase like a cavern carved out of red natural stone. The staircase brings visitors to a first lookout into the heart of the greenhouses, literally cutting a corner from the floor plan to do so, before it reaches the roof of the visitor pavilion between the greenhouse roofs. An arched vault clad in stone rises above the glass landscape, protruding from the roof terrace. Beneath it is a panoramic interior with space for exhibitions, workshops and receptions, and which also provides unobstructed views into the inner workings of plant research.

Bernard Rudofsky's tectonics and vernacular poetry reverberate in the dome of the Green Ark, a hyperbolic paraboloid. The hyperbole makes a visit to the Botanic Garden memorable. Not through decorative excess, but through sober yet impressive design and an authentic spatial experience. Around the spectacle of the central wooden vault, concrete pillars outline a rigid circular walkway that generously leaves space for the plant collection. The same down-to-earth concrete structure is deployed at the garden's entrance pavilion, where NU has crossed two rows of T-elements to redraw relations between reception, ticket desk, shop, park and a multi-purpose former farmhouse. The cross shape delineates a public forecourt, redraws the line between inside and outside, and unites interior, architecture and landscape in one open structure. One arm extends into the botanical garden as a horizontal platform, making the slightly sloping site legible. Instead of stepping to the fore, the architecture, like a soft filter, enhances the experience of the landscape.

Part of the World

For a lookout point at the former carp-breeding ponds of Bellefroid near Leuven, NU went one step further by literally setting to work with the surrounding landscape. Together with the landscape architects of Overlant, they built a 'fauna fort' with a porous outer shell, constructed from the various layers of earth in the area, like a local geological sample sheet. The erosion at work – which varies according to the composition of each layer – determines the ultimate shape of the retaining structure. NU set out the basic rules of the design but ultimately let nature take its course. This is also the case throughout the nature domain, which is committed to restoring an unspoilt nature and will be partially inaccessible. The crevices, holes and protrusions of the lookout are an informal addition to this habitat. The fort belongs to the local fauna and flora. Humans are temporary guests, there for a nice view or a short night.

With the fauna fort, the experiments from the early days got a current, climate-conscious update. Polyesters and moulds for concrete have evolved into eroding layers of earth and ecosystems. Engineers and other specialists got drawn into the quest for an end

result that lies invariably outside the comfort zone. Their specific knowledge of the details makes possible the shared ambition of the project. Exactly how this will happen is rarely clear at the start, but there is great confidence in the process. The competition proposal for an outdoor swimming pool in the Vaartkom in Leuven is the next logical step in this. NU and landscaping office Omgeving consciously chose, not for a hard spatial intervention, but for the optimization of the place as it is, by making the water of the Vaartkom itself swimmable. A long-term sustainable process is at the core of the submitted proposal. By improving the city's water quality year after year, a project is created for all the people of Leuven with added value for the neighbourhood.

A similar intention lies behind the conversion of the International Congress Center in Ghent, in collaboration with Brussels-based 51N4E. The ICC is part of an extensive cluster of buildings in the middle of Citadelpark that includes the Municipal Museum of Contemporary Art (S.M.A.K.) and the legendary indoor cycling track 't Kuipke. At the heart of the cluster is the impressive Floraliënhal, which is opened up to give the park the breathing space it needs. This creates a generous surface for communal use at the heart of both the park and the city. A binding design gives way to profound confidence in the potential of the available space. Small landscape elements are added that can be used freely for various purposes, with each making their own place in a larger collective whole by means of small gestures.

During a stay in a forest cabin in Sweden, Halewijn made a linocut depicting how he relates to the world. In the foreground, we see the designer's sketching hand, close to his own thinking and making. The eye then moves to the others, a community around a campfire. It is a relation marked by tension, between togetherness and the individual cocoon. Behind the fire, the landscape appears, the place where we live. Beyond that, the starry sky, the depths of the universe. These are layers that seem to exist separately, Halewijn argues, different perspectives from which to look at the same thing, each step appearing to trivialize the previous one. But it is precisely these leaps in scale, and their interconnections, that define the richness of an environment.

The drawing can be seen as a map to NU's oeuvre, testifying to the architects' typical eagerness to constantly dive into new domains and open them up with their architecture. Armand and Halewijn explore the world together through their projects – fuelled by one's fascination for pared-down structures and by the other's urge for scope and mass – not from a flawless plan, but from a keen process gradually involving more and more people and disciplines.

Understanding things – programme, people, material – is what drives NU's practice. This spirit of discovery also ensures that the office cannot be reduced to one typical architectural style. Each new staircase is a surprise, each new project grows out of its specific place and content. By reducing things to their essence but also giving them substance, NU creates sincere architecture, free of cynicism. Light and heavy at the same time.

LINQ
NEW HOUSE/OFFICE

Sint-Denijs-Westrem, 2006
In collaboration with: Arunas Arlauskas
Engineering: Babel (stability)

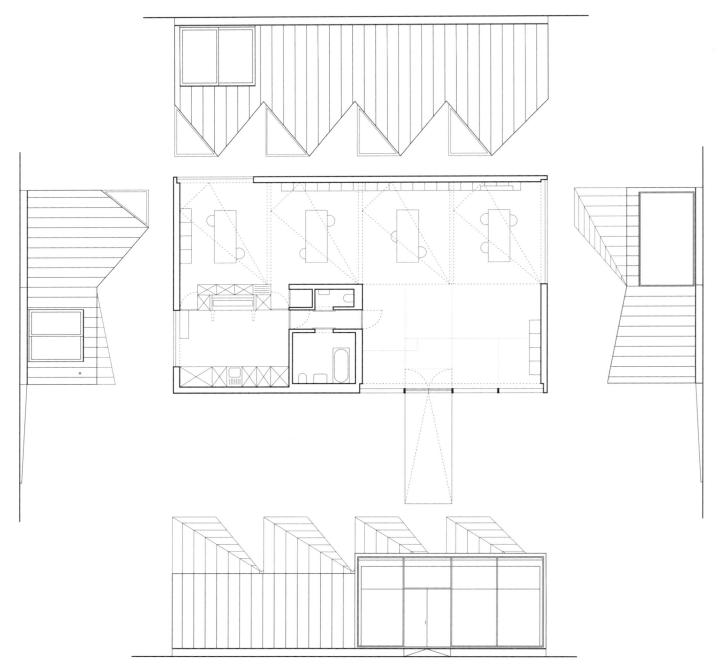

HUIS PERREKES
CARE HOME
CONVERSION/RENOVATION AS-NEW

Oosterlo, 2018
Client: Huis Perrekes vzw
In collaboration with: Ester Goris (project management), Plant en Houtgoed (landscape)
Engineering: Infrabo NV (stability, techniques and EPB), De Fonseca (acoustics)

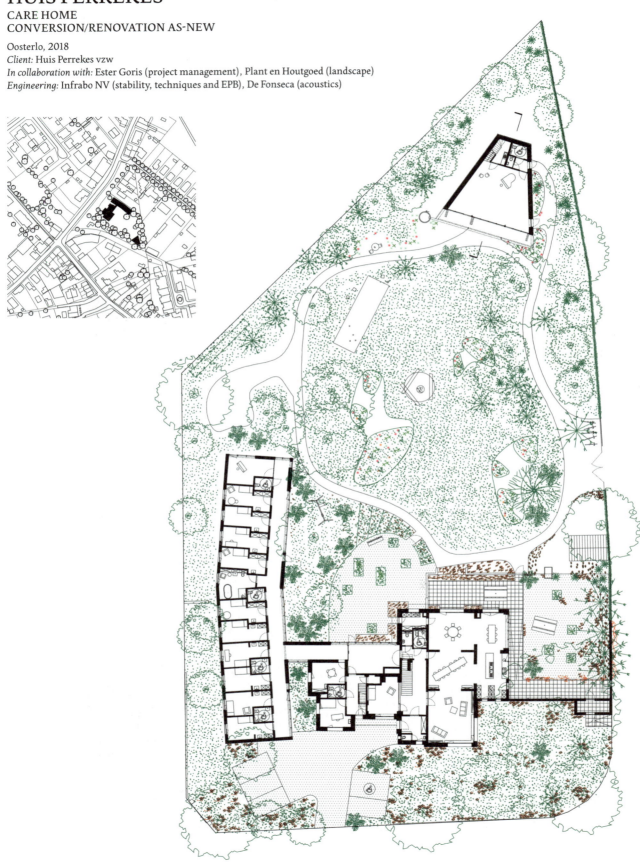

Groundlevel and garden

Front façade

Back façade

Section Pavilion · Façade Pavilion

0 2   10 m

175

177

EMILIANI
NEW CONSTRUCTION AND RENOVATION OF VILLA INTO CARE HOMES

Zaffelare (Lochristi), ongoing
Client: Emiliani vzw
In collaboration with: Jan Minne (landscape)
Engineering: Fraeye (stability), Boydens (techniques)

Ground level

JOSEPH BRACOPS HOSPITAL
MASTER PLAN AND NEW HOSPITAL

Anderlecht, ongoing
Client: Hôpitaux Iris Sud
In collaboration with: Archipelago, Buur
Engineering: MC² (stability), Ellipse (techniques), Matriciel (sustainability)

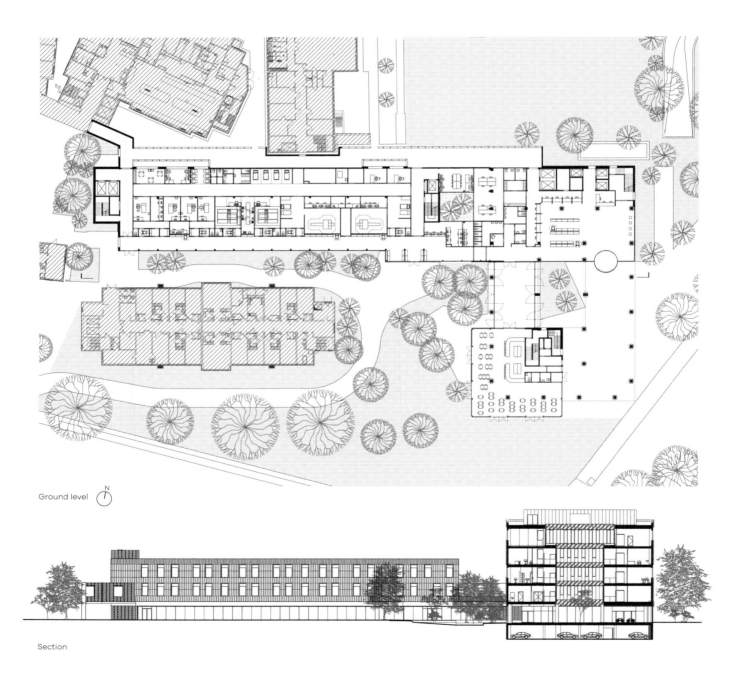

Ground level

Section

East façade

ZEVENBERGEN SERVICES CENTRE
CONVERSION/RENOVATION AS-NEW OF CARE HOMES

Ranst, ongoing (phase 2 of 3 executed, phase 3 in preliminary design)
Client: Dagverzorgingscentrum (DVC) Zevenbergen
In collaboration with: AA Pierre Hebbelinck Pierre de Wit (concept phase)
Engineering: Robuust (stability and techniques)

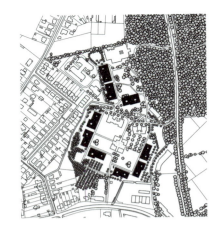

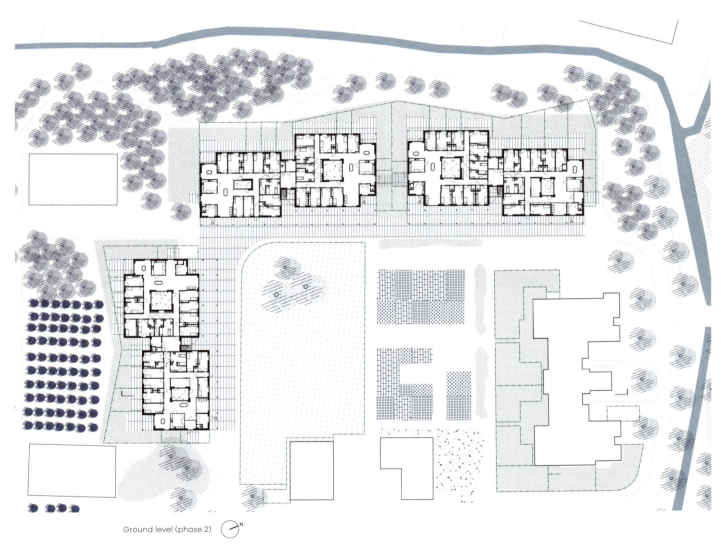

Ground level (phase 2)

Section (phase 2)

BOMASTRAAT
NEW HOUSE

Ghent, 2009
Engineering: Fraeye (stability)

HEILIG HART COLLEGE WAREGEM
SCHOOL EXTENSION AND PLAYGROUND REDESIGN

Waregem, 2019
Client: Campus College Waregem
In collaboration with: AA Pierre Hebbelinck
Pierre De Wit (design phase)
Engineering: Robuust (stability and techniques)

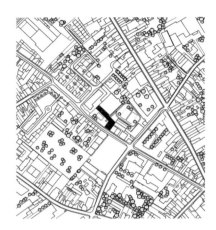

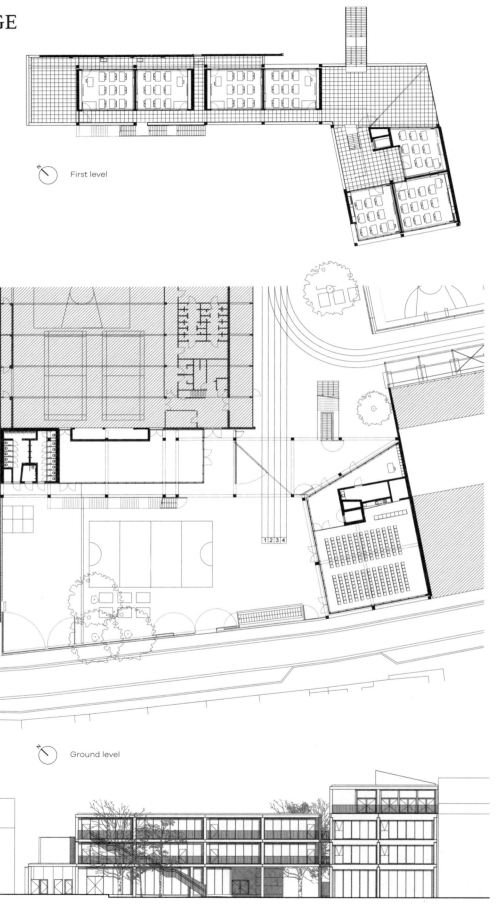

BAGATTENSTRAAT
NEW TERRACED HOUSE WITH STUDIO SPACE

Ghent, 2019
In collaboration with: Atelier Arne Deruyter (garden)
Engineering: Jan Hoste (stability), HP Engineering (techniques)

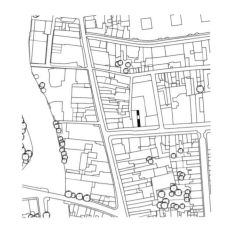

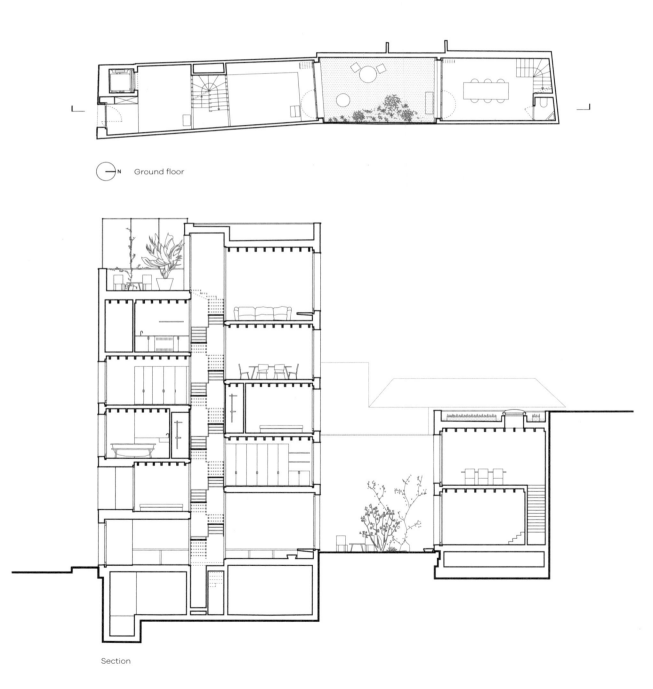

Ground floor

Section

ICC
CONVERSION AND RESTORATION OF THE INTERNATIONAL CONVENTION CENTER (ICC)

Ghent, ongoing
In collaboration with: 51N4E, Plant en Houtgoed, Altstadt
Engineering: Bollinger+Grohmann (stability), Ingenium (techniques), Kahle (acoustics), ELD (cost consult), Jonckheere (infrastructure), FESG (fire engineering)

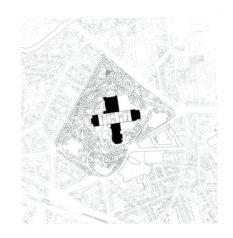

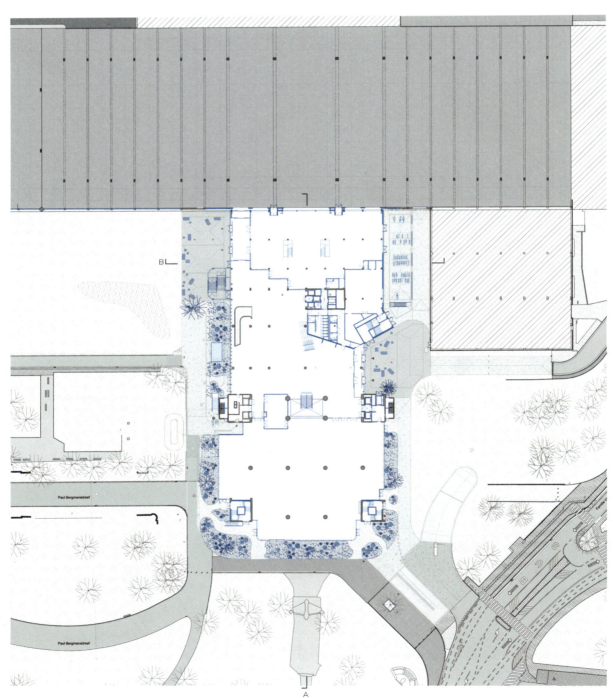

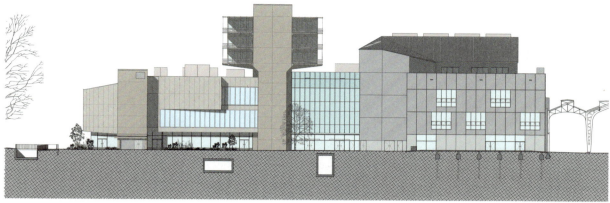
East façade

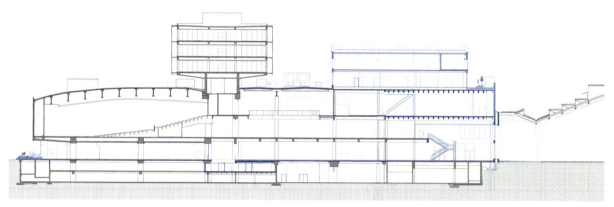
Section A

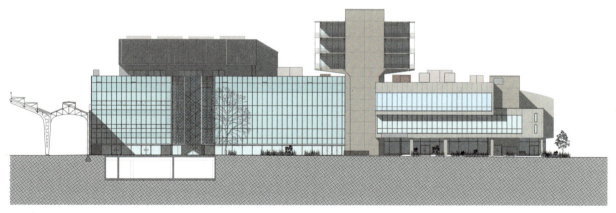
West façade

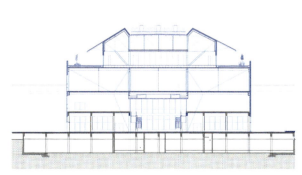
Section B

Façade Floraliënhal

LANDSKOUTER
NEW HOUSE

Landskouter, 2014
Engineering: Engitop (stability)

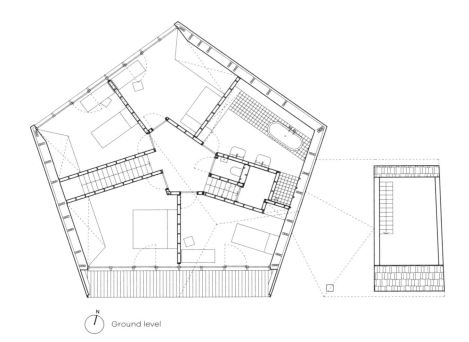

Ground level

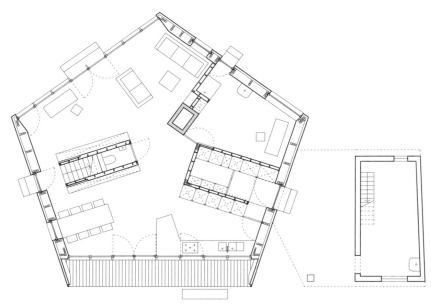

First level

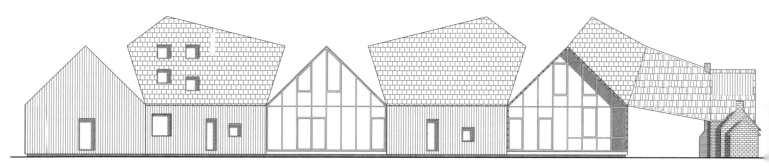

Façades

MEISE BOTANIC GARDEN RECEPTION
NEW CONSTRUCTION, CONVERSION OF RECEPTION BUILDING

Meise, 2021
Client: Agentschap Plantentuin Meise
In collaboration with: Archipelago, Ar-te, Arne Deruyter (landscape)
Engineering: Mouton (stability), Boydens (techniques)

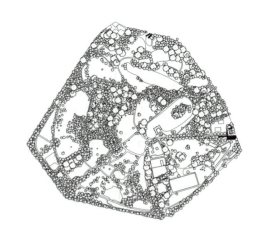

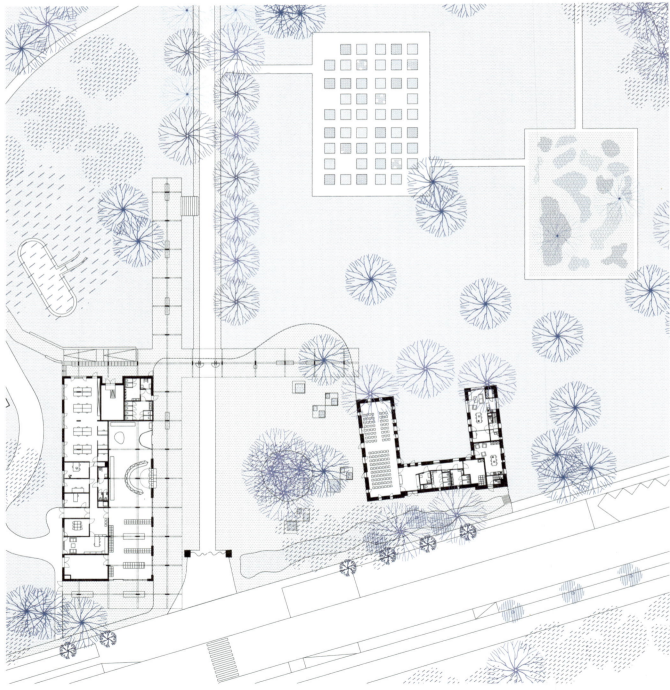

Main entrance

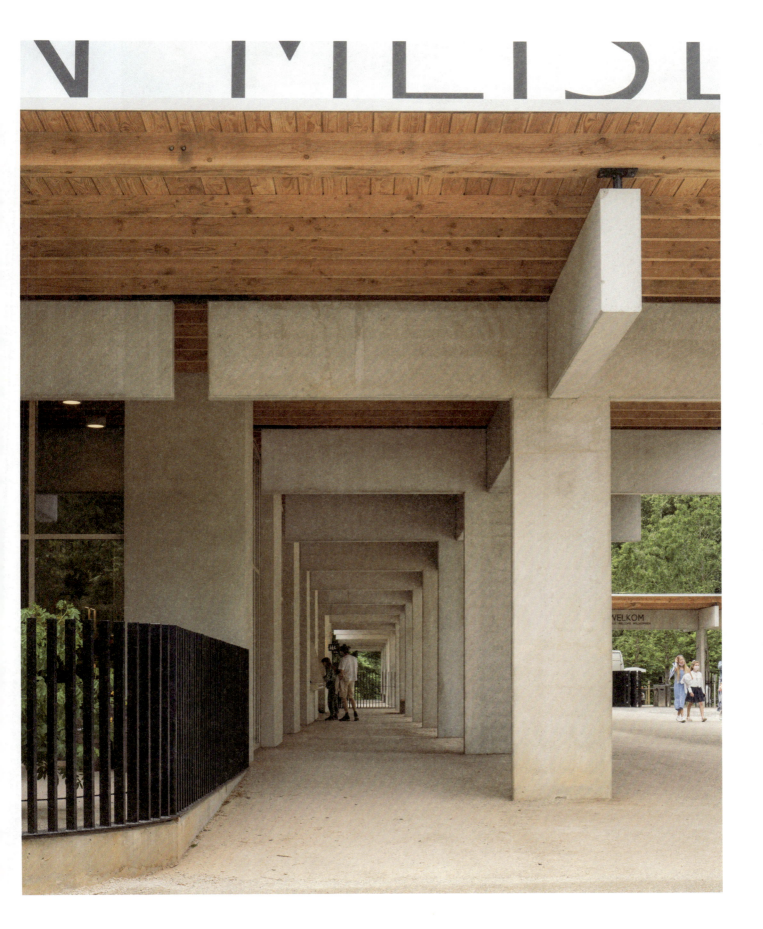

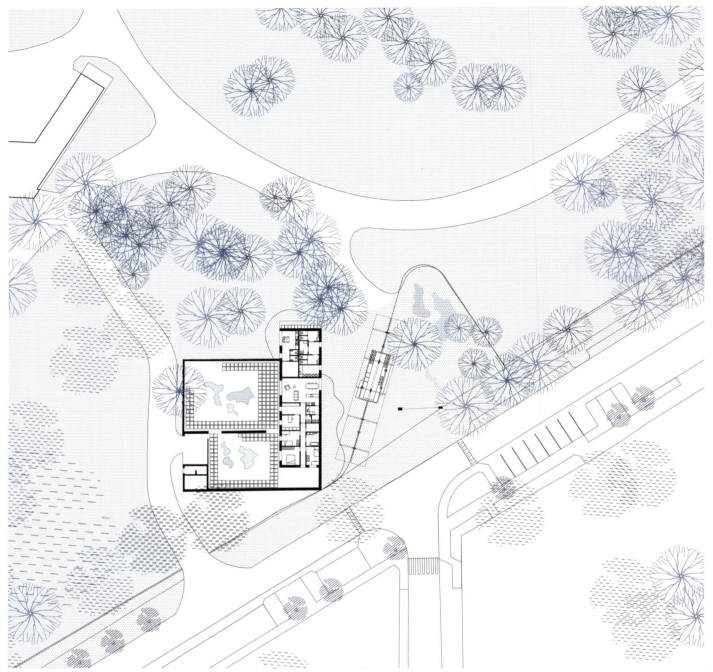

Entrance Meise

MEISE BOTANIC GARDEN GREEN ARK
GREENHOUSES, VISITOR PAVILION, SERVICES BUILDING

Meise, ongoing
Client: Agentschap Plantentuin Meise
In collaboration with: Archipelago, Frans Zwinkels (greenhouse construction), Plant en Houtgoed (landscape)
Engineering: Mouton (stability), Boydens (techniques)

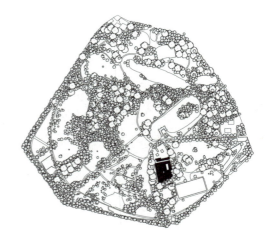

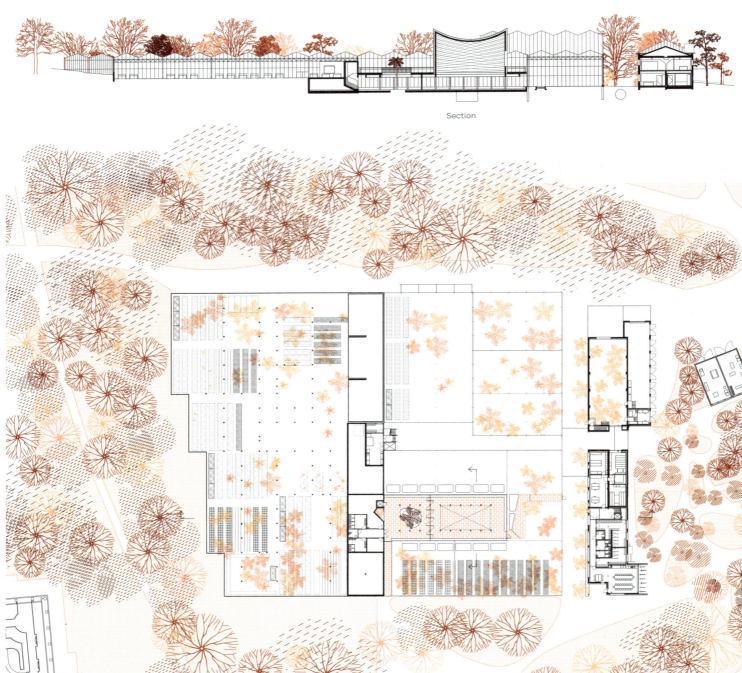

Section

Ground level

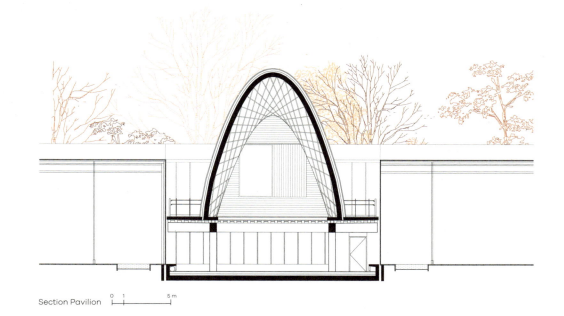

Section Pavilion 0 1 5 m

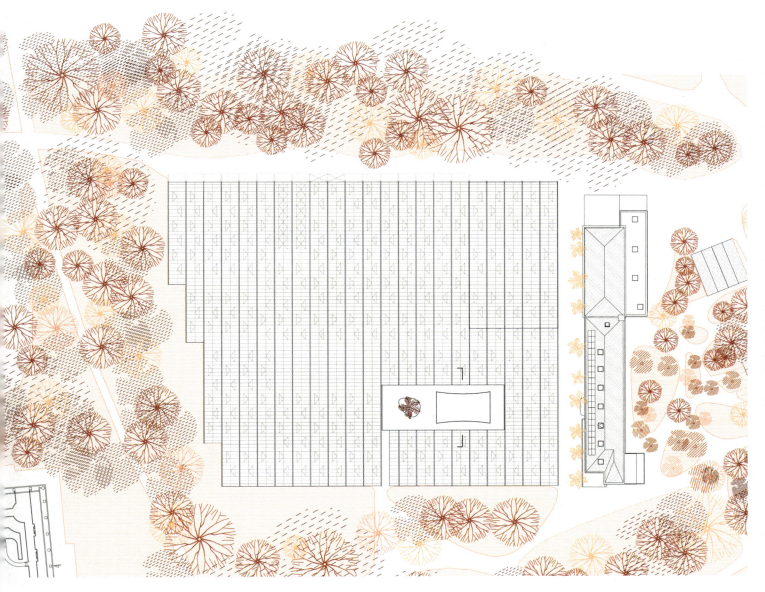

Roof plan

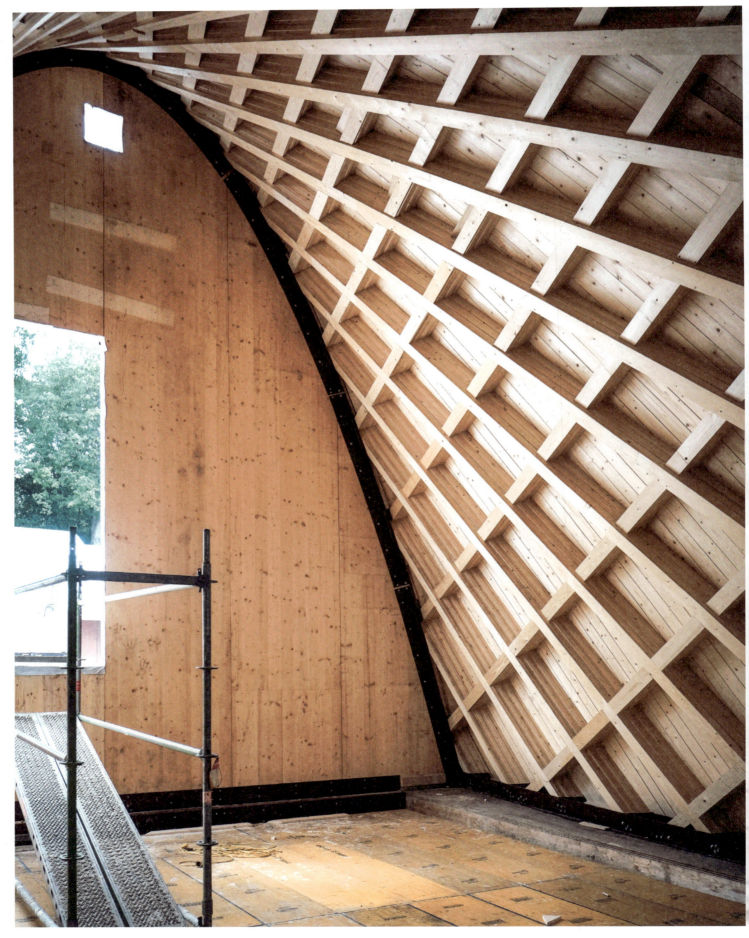

PROJECT LIST
NU architectuuratelier
(Chronological)

Halvemaanstraat
House renovation
Sint-Amandsberg (Ghent), 2003

Korenbloemstraat
House conversion
Ghent, 2004 (phase 1) – 2011 (phase 2)

First table
Table, 2005
Client: Linq

Mathilde
House renovation
Ledeberg, 2005

Xi
House conversion
Ghent, 2005

Jean-Paul Laenen
Exhibition scenography
Mechelen, 2005
Client: Lamot
In collaboration with: Arunas Arlauskas

Art Academy
Tienen, 2006 *(competition design)*
Client: Municipality of Tienen

Theater Victoria
Master plan and theatre house renovation
Ghent, 2006
Client: Theater Victoria

Linq
New house/office
Sint-Denijs-Westrem, 2006
In collaboration with: Arunas Arlauskas
Engineering: Babel (stability)

Boxy
Bathroom cell
Sint-Martens-Latem, 2006

Bulo folding screen
Modular folding screen (study)
Mechelen, 2006
Client: Bulo

De Wissel
Community centre renovation
Bruges, 2006
Client: De Wissel vzw

Biennale Interieur
Event scenography
Kortrijk, 2006
Client: Stichting Interieur
In collaboration with: Doorzon interieurarchitecten

35m³ young architecture
Exhibition
Antwerp, 2006
Client: Flanders Architecture Institute

Dave and Lisa
House renovation
Ghent, 2007

Vredestraat
House renovation
Ghent, 2007

Abrahamstraat
House conversion
Ghent, 2007
In collaboration with: Doorzon interieurarchitecten

Boudewijnstraat
Renovation of houses
Ghent, 2008

Venice Biennale
Exhibition concept Belgian Pavilion
Venice, 2008 *(competition design)*

ORDOS 100
New villa
Ordos (China), 2008 *(design phase)*

Diamond District
Public space security infrastructure
Antwerp, 2008 *(competition design)*
Client: Antwerp World Diamond Centre (AWDC)

Esplanadestraat
House renovation
Aalst, 2009

Bomastraat
New house
Ghent, 2009
Engineering: Fraeye (stability)

Kessel-Lo
Renovation of single-family house with studio
Kessel-Lo, 2009
Engineering: Arthur De Roover (stability)

Second table
Table, 2009

Container parks
Antwerp, 2009 *(competition design)*
Client: City of Antwerp
In association with: Kris Coremans
Engineering: Arthur De Roover (stability),
HP Engineers (techniques)

Gordunakaai
House
Ghent, 2009 (concept phase)

Voka
Offices
Ghent, 2009 *(competition design)*
Client: Voka Oost-Vlaanderen

Gasometers
Repurposing of gasometers
Ghent, 2009 *(concept phase)*
Client: Canal Properties, Vanhaerents, Vooruitzicht

Boat kitchen
Kitchen
Ghent, 2009 *(concept phase)*

Honeycomb
Panel
Lissewege, 2009

Manchester building
Industrial heritage building conversion
Ghent, 2010 *(design phase)*
Engineering and restoration: Util (stability), Sabine Okkerse (restoration)

Nederpolder
Rooftop flat
Ghent, 2010
In collaboration with: Doorzon interieurarchitecten

Magazine Club
Nightclub
Lille (FR), 2010
Client: Musik Prod

Vooruit
Arts centre renovation
Ghent, 2010 *(competition design)*
Client: Vooruit Gent
Engineering: Arthur De Roover (stability),
HP Engineers (techniques)

De Motte
Residential development and renovation
Ghent, 2010– ongoing
Client: Acasa

Green roads
Master vision and design of cycling roads
West Flanders, 2011
Client: Westtoer
In partnership with: Tractebel-Technum (infrastructure)

Baelskaai
Residential development
Ostend, 2011 *(concept phase)*
Client: Vanhaerents
In collaboration with: Architecten Achtergael, Office 360

Satijnstraat
House conversion
Ghent, 2011

Crematorium Zemst
New crematorium
Zemst-Eppegem, 2011 *(competition design)*
Client: Havicrem
In collaboration with: Karel Bruylandt,
Kris Coremans
Engineering: HP Engineers (stability),
Cobe (techniques)

Atelier Bouwmeester
Furnishing the workshop of the Team Flemish Government Architect
Ravenstein Gallery, Brussels, 2011
Client: Team Flemish Government Architect
In collaboration with: Nick Top

Leeuw
New house
Sint-Pieters-Leeuw, 2012
Engineering: Robuust (stability and techniques)

Tentoonstellingslaan
House conversion
Ghent, 2012
Engineering: Engitop (stability)

Jan Verspeyenstraat
Studio, house and gallery
Ghent, 2012 *(design phase)*

Oude Dokken
Residential development
Ghent, 2012 *(competition design)*
Client: Willemen Real Estate, DMI Vastgoed
In collaboration with: Buur, Kempe Thill, Sergison Bates, Atelier Bow-Wow, HUB, Bureau Bas Smets

De Porre
Feasibility study
Ghent, 2012
Client: sogent

Kattevennen Cosmodrome
Master plan for astronomic centre
Genk, 2012 *(competition design)*
Client: City of Genk

C-mine Expedition
Architectural route, scenography
Genk, 2012 (opening) - 2019 (expansion)
Client: City of Genk
In collaboration with: Kabvis (Mathilde Geens),
Ruben Nachtergaele
Engineering: Grontmij / Sweco (support for execution, stability and techniques)

Sint-Lucas light bricks
Plastic bricks
Ghent, 2013
In collaboration with: Xaveer De Geyter Architects
Client: LUCA School of Arts

Wellness
Nijlen, 2013 *(concept phase)*

Oude Houtlei
House conversion
Ghent, 2013

Jan Portaels Hospital
New hospital
Vilvoorde, 2013 *(design phase)*
Client: AZ Jan Portaels
In association with: Archipelago, Gortemaker Algra
Feenstra, West 8
Engineering: Daidalos Peutz (sustainability),
Macobo-Stabo (stability and techniques)

Scheldelei reception site
Outlook tower
Kruibeke, 2013 *(competition design)*
Client: Agency for Nature and Forests
Engineering: Grontmij/Sweco (stability and techniques)

Mother
Bar, restaurant
Lille (FR), 2013
Client: Musik Prod

Groot Schijn Park
Park and sports infrastructure
Antwerp, 2013 *(competition design)*
Client: Antwerp City Planning
In collaboration with: Tractebel-Technum (infrastructure), Erik De Waele (landscape)
Engineering: i.m.d.c. (water infrastructure)

Stukatelier
Co-housing house conversion
Ghent, 2014
In collaboration with: Mieke Van der Linden

Landskouter
New house
Landskouter, 2014
Engineering: Engitop (stability)

Emiel
House conversion
Ghent, 2014

Pilot project Sint-Anna
Master plan pilot project invisible care (Flemish Government Architect)
Sint-Truiden, 2014
Client: Sint-Anna vzw
In collaboration with: Archipelago, Stefaan Thiers and Denis Dujardin (landscape), Maarten Loopmans, Tine Buffel, Tinie Kardol, a2o (residential development phase)
Engineering: Macobo-Stabo (stability and techniques)

Operaplein info pavilion
Temporary pavilion
Antwerp, 2014 *(competition design)*
Client: City of Antwerp
Engineering: Robuust (stability and techniques)

East Flanders Provincial Government Building
Renovation of former barracks into provincial government building and housing
Ghent, 2014 *(competition design)*
Client: Province of East Flanders
In association with: AA Pierre Hebbelinck Pierre De Wit, Aldrik Heirman
Engineering: Daidalos Peutz (sustainability), Greisch (stability), Boydens (techniques)

Mundus building
Imaginary building, 2014
Client: Christophe Van Gerrewey

Haeck
House
Sint-Martens-Latem, 2015
Engineering: Arthur De Roover (stability)

Lierneux
New house with guest house
Lierneux, 2015
In collaboration with: He-architectes

Bank van de Arbeid
Design of reception and exhibition area
Ghent, 2015
Client: sogent
In collaboration with: Kabvis (Mathilde Geens)

Masseria Gantoise
House
Puglia (IT), 2015

Karel Mirystraat
House conversion
Ghent, 2015

Stijn and Mathilde
House conversion
Ghent, 2015

Picardy
Penthouse apartment added to block of flats
Knokke, 2016
Engineering: Arcade (stability), HP Engineers (techniques)

Pilot project Productive Landscape
Innovative greenhouse complex
Roeselare, 2016 *(competition design)*
Client: Inagro vzw
In collaboration with: Archipelago, Lateral Thinking Factory, Frans Zwinkels
Engineering: Macobo-Stabo (stability and techniques)

East Flanders Provincial Government Building
Renovation of former barracks into provincial government building and housing
Ghent, 2016 *(competition design)*
Client: Province of East Flanders (via Willemen Real Estate DBFM)
In collaboration with: Architecten Achtergael, aNNo
Engineering: TPF (techniques), D2S (acoustics)

Bergbos
Multi-family house
Merelbeke, 2017
Client: Artenys

Le Babe
Bar, restaurant
Lille (FR), 2017
Client: Musik Prod

Zonnelied
Care site master plan
Roosdaal, 2017
Client: Zonnelied vzw
In collaboration with: 1010 Architecture Urbanism

Saint-Luc University Hospital
Hospital renovation and new construction
Brussels, 2017
Client: Cliniques Universitaires Saint-Luc
In collaboration with: Archipelago, Pargade, Buur
Engineering: Arcadis (stability), Apsis (techniques)

Church of the Sacred Heart
Repurposing of church and presbytery into neighbourhood centre, public space
Sint-Amandsberg (Ghent), 2017 *(competition design)*
Client: sogent
In collaboration with: Buur
Engineering: Boydens (techniques), Util (stability), Erik Geens (cost consultancy), France (water management)

Pompentoren
Outlook tower
Eernegem, 2017 *(competition design)*
Client: Province of West Flanders, Westtoer
Engineering: Mouton (stability), Boydens (techniques)

Concertgebouw Brugge
Visitor scenography and reception redesign
Bruges, 2017
Client: Concertgebouw Brugge
In collaboration with: Kabvis (Mathilde Geens) (scenography and graphics), Ruben Nachtergaele (sound), Ester Goris (curtain), Heleen van Haegenborgh (composition), Roo Se (sound model)

Huis Perrekes
Care home conversion/renovation as-new
Oosterlo, 2018
Client: Huis Perrekes vzw
In collaboration with: Ester Goris (project management), Plant en Houtgoed (landscape)
Engineering: Infrabo NV (stability, techniques and EPB), De Fonseca (acoustics)

Belval
Public space and repurposing industrial heritage
Esch-sur-Alzette (Luxembourg), 2018 *(competition design)*
Client: Agora & Cie
In collaboration with: Studio SNCDA
Engineering: Bollinger+Grohmann (stability), Betic (techniques)

Breughel
Scenography
Bokrijk, 2018 *(competition design)*
Client: Het Domein Bokrijk
In collaboration with: Kabvis (Mathilde Geens)

Windhouse
House
Yell, Shetland Islands, Scotland, 2018 *(design phase)*

HSC Gasthuisberg
Master plan and partial assignments public space hospital
Leuven, 2018
Client: Health Sciences campus Gasthuisberg

Sint-Jozef Sint-Pieter School
Secondary school
Blankenberge, 2018 *(competition design)*
Client: Sint-Jozef Sint-Pieter
In collaboration with: Label
Engineering: Ingenium (techniques), Cobe (stability)

Bagattenstraat
New terraced house with studio space
Ghent, 2019
In collaboration with: Atelier Arne Deruyter (garden)
Engineering: Jan Hoste (stability), HP Engineers (techniques)

Neerschelde
Multi-family house
Ghent, 2019
Client: sogent, private client
Engineering: Arthur De Roover (stability), HP Engineers (techniques)

Heilig Hart College Waregem
School extension and playground redesign
Waregem, 2019
Client: Campus College Waregem
In collaboration with: AA Pierre Hebbelinck Pierre De Wit (design phase)
Engineering: Robuust (stability and techniques)

Sinaai
House conversion
Sinaai, 2019

Watersnip
Master plan site development
Koersel, 2019
Client: Province of Limburg
In collaboration with: Omgeving

Britney
Bar, restaurant
Lille (FR), 2019
Client: Musik Prod

C-mine Expedition story cones
Scenography
Genk, 2019
Client: City of Genk
In collaboration with: Kabvis (Mathilde Geens)

Kaaitheater
Theatre conversion
Brussels, 2019 (competition design)
Client: Flemish Community
In collaboration with: CRIT., Gideon Boie
Engineering: Chevalier Masson (interiors), TTAS (theatre techniques), Mouton (stability), Ingenium (techniques), Kahle (acoustics), Daidalos Peutz (special studies)

Les Marronniers
New psychiatric centre
Tournai, 2019 *(competition design)*
Client: Centre Régional Psychiatrique Les Marronniers
In collaboration with: de vylder vinck taillieu, Studio SNCDA, Constructivas, Taktyk
Engineering: Boydens (techniques), Bollinger+Grohmann (stability), Daidalos Peutz (acoustics), Delta-GC (techniques)
Experts: Martin Vandenende, Johanna Broeckaert, BAVO

Sint-Jan Hospital
Master plan for the hospital public space
Brussels, 2019
Client: Kliniek Sint-Jan

Steiner School
New school building
Ghent, 2019 *(competition design)*
Client: Vrije Rudolf Steinerschool, Ghent

Kattevennen Stokkenmanroute
Landscape scenography
Genk, 2020
Client: Kattevennen vzw
In collaboration with: Kabvis (Mathilde Geens)

Jessa Hospital
New hospital and landscape design
Hasselt, 2020 *(competition design)*
Client: Jessa Ziekenhuis
In collaboration with: Polo, Archipelago, 1010 Architecture Urbanism, Jan Minne (landscape)
Engineering: Ingenium (techniques), Mouton (stability), Constructivas (care consult), Greenspot (environment)

Hagelstein
Sports hall
Sint-Katelijne-Waver, 2020 *(phase building permit)*
Client: Kitos vzw
Engineering: Boydens (techniques), Fraeye (stability), De Fonseca (acoustics)

Meise Botanic Garden logistics
Logistics buildings
Meise, 2020 (competition design)
Client: Agentschap Plantentuin Meise
In collaboration with: Archipelago, Altstadt, Plant en Houtgoed
Engineering: Boydens (techniques), Mouton (stability)

Vaartkom
Public space
Leuven, 2020 (competition design)
Client: City of Leuven
In collaboration with: Omgeving, François Antoine
Engineering: Navicula (aquatic biology)

De Lovie
New care homes
Poperinge, 2020 (competition design)
Client: De Lovie vzw
In collaboration with: Sabine Okkerse (restoration)
Engineering: Boydens (techniques)

Alien
Bar, restaurant
Lille (FR), 2021
Client: Musik Prod

Villa Joseph
Vision development cohousing and care
Lubbeek, 2021

Prosperhoeve
Master plan repurposing of historic farmstead
Beveren, 2021
Client: Municipality of Beveren
In collaboration with: Omgeving, Orientes

Citadelpark
Building cluster master plan
Ghent, 2021
Client: sogent
In collaboration with: 51N4E
Engineering: Ingenium (techniques), Bollinger+Grohmann (stability), Altstadt (restoration)

Meise Botanic Garden reception
New construction, conversion of reception building
Meise, 2021
Client: Agentschap Plantentuin Meise
In collaboration with: Archipelago, Ar-te, Arne Deruyter (landscape)
Engineering: Mouton (stability), Boydens (techniques)

Meise Botanic Garden welcome garden
Garden layout
Meise, 2021
Client: Agentschap Plantentuin Meise
In collaboration with: Arne De Ruyter (landscape)

Mich and Marieke
House conversion
Ghent, 2022

La Maillerie
Bar, restaurant
Lille (FR), 2022
Client: Musik Prod

Swam
Bar, restaurant
Lille (FR), 2022
Client: Musik Prod

S.M.A.K.
Feasibility study Museum of Contemporary Art
Ghent, 2022
Client: sogent
In collaboration with: 51N4E
Engineering: Ingenium (techniques), Bollinger+Grohmann (stability)

Sea Tower Expedition
Water tower conversion
Koksijde, 2022 (competition design)
Client: Intermunicipal water company of Veurne-Ambacht – Aquaduin
In collaboration with: Bleau Climbing Team, Kabvis (Mathilde Geens)
Engineering: Mouton (stability), Boydens (techniques), Kahle (acoustics)

Bekaert site Hemiksem
Residential development
Hemiksem, 2022 *(competition design)*
Client: Park aan de Stroom II
In collaboration with: HUB, Felt, Overlant (landscape)

De Zande
Youth detention centre
Ruislede, 2022 *(competition design)*
Client: Community institution De Zande
In collaboration with: Jan Minne (landscape)-
Engineering: Fraeye (stability), Boydens (techniques)

De Vlieger
School and childcare centre renovation
Ghent, 2022 *(competition design)*
Client: City of Ghent
In collaboration with: Atelier voor groene ruimte
Engineering: Fraeye (stability), Tech3 (techniques)

Hoboken
Local services centre, 66 service flats
Hoboken, 2022
Client: Zorgbedrijf Antwerpen (via DBFM Democo)
In collaboration with: Archipelago

Commandry Gruitrode
Master plan and scenographic renovation of historic site
Oudsbergen, ongoing
Client: Municipality of Oudsbergen
In collaboration with: Kabvis (Mathilde Geens), Michel Janssen, BuroLandschap (landscape)

Labland Retail-Housing
Research living above commercial premises
Zottegem, 2023
Client: Labland

De Boomgaard
New housing units with care aspect and neighbourhood operation
Leuven, 2023 *(competition design)*
Client: Livez
In collaboration with: Plant en Houtgoed
Engineering: Engelen (stability), Infrabo (techniques), De Fonseca (acoustics)

Rivierenhof technical centre
Logistics centre
Antwerp, 2023 *(competition design)*
Client: Provincial authorities of Antwerp
In collaboration with: Archipelago, Michel Pauwels (landscape)
Engineering: VDS (environmental consultancy), DS engineering (techniques), Atelier-T (stability)

Vlinderhof
Care homes for people with disabilities
Biezenmortel (NL), ongoing
Client: Prisma
In collaboration with: Bureau Eau (execution)
Engineering: Klictet (installations and techniques), Goudstikker De Vries (stability), Cauberghuygen (acoustics)

Zevenbergen services centre
Conversion/renovation as-new of care homes
Ranst, ongoing (phase 2 of 3 executed, phase 3 in preliminary design)
Client: Dagverzorgingscentrum (DVC) Zevenbergen
In collaboration with: AA Pierre Hebbelinck Pierre de Wit (concept phase)
Engineering: Robuust (stability and techniques)

11.11.11
Renovation of offices and layout of outdoor space
Brussels, ongoing
Client: 11.11.11 vzw
In collaboration with: Intro (landscape)
Engineering: Pieter Lootens (EPB), Lambda-max (stability)

Cradle bed
Furniture design
Ongoing
Initiative: NU and Huis Perrekes

Meise Botanic Garden Green Ark
Greenhouses, visitor pavilion, services building
Meise, ongoing
Client: Agentschap Plantentuin Meise
In collaboration with: Archipelago, Frans Zwinkels (greenhouse construction), Plant en Houtgoed (landscape)
Engineering: Mouton (stability), Boydens (techniques)

Joseph Bracops Hospital
Master plan and new hospital
Anderlecht, ongoing
Client: Hôpitaux Iris Sud
In collaboration with: Archipelago, Buur
Engineering: MC² (stability), Ellipse (techniques), Matriciel (sustainability)

ICC
Conversion and restoration of the International Convention Center (ICC)
Ghent, ongoing
Client: Citadel Finance
In collaboration with: 51N4E, Plant en Houtgoed
Engineering: Bollinger+Grohmann (stability), Ingenium (techniques), Altstadt (restoration), Kahle (acoustics), ELD (cost consult), Jonckheere (infrastructure), FESG (fire engineering)

Centers
Renovation of spaces under railway arches
Borgerhout, 2018 (phase 2 ongoing)
Client: AG Vespa
Engineering: Boydens (techniques), Jan Hoste (stability)

Meise Botanic Garden farmstead
Renovation and new construction of farmstead and restoration of castle
Meise, ongoing
Client: Agentschap Plantentuin Meise
In collaboration with: Archipelago, Altstadt, Plant en Houtgoed
Engineering: Mouton (stability), Boydens (techniques)

Emiliani
New construction and renovation of villa into care homes
Zaffelare (Lochristi), ongoing
Client: Emiliani vzw
In collaboration with: Jan Minne (landscape)
Engineering: Fraeye (stability), Boydens (techniques)

Meise Botanic Garden parking
Landscape design and parking infrastructure
Meise, ongoing
Client: Agentschap Plantentuin Meise
In collaboration with: Omgeving
Engineering: bDA-plan (infrastructure), Boydens (techniques), Mouton (stability)

Kessel care centre
Residential care centre with services centre and landscape design
Kessel, ongoing
Client: Zusters van Berlaar
In partnership with: Raamwerk, Plusoffice, Plant en Houtgoed
Engineering: Ingenium (techniques), ELD (stability and consultancy), Ara (environment)

Church of Anzegem
Village space
Anzegem, ongoing
Client: Municipality of Anzegem
In collaboration with: Jan Minne (landscape)
Engineering and heritage: Lime (stability), Sabine Okkerse (heritage)

Genk-Kattevennen landscape connection
Landscape vision and spatial interventions
Genk, ongoing
Client: City of Genk
In collaboration with: Overlant (landscape)

Bellefroid Ponds
Landscape design and natural infrastructure
Leuven, ongoing
Client: City of Leuven
In collaboration with: Overlant (landscape)
Engineering: Mieco Effect (environment), Plot (spatial management), Erasmus Hogeschool, Kenniscentrum Tuin, France (infrastructure)

Heers Castle
Castle site development strategy
Heers, ongoing
Client: Herita
In collaboration with: Overlant (landscape), Sabine Okkerse (restoration)
Experts: Idea Consult, HO Gent, Anneleen Cassiman, Mieco Effect

Planet Path Kattevennen
Educational landscape scenography
Genk, ongoing
Client: Kattevennen vzw, City of Genk
In collaboration with: Kabvis (Mathilde Geens)

North-South artworks
Bridges and ecoducts
Limburg, ongoing
Client: DWZ
In collaboration with: Maat-ontwerpers, 51N4E
Engineering: Tractebel-Technum (infrastructure), Arcadis (stability)

Nieuwenhoven castle domain
Master plan and new reception building
Sint-Truiden, ongoing
Client: Province of Limburg
In collaboration with: Dethier (design and build), BuroLandschap (landscape)
Engineering: V2S (stability), Boydens (techniques)

BIOGRAPHY

NU architectuuratelier was founded in 2004 by Armand Eeckels (b. 1973), Halewijn Lievens (b. 1975) and Arúnas Arlauskas (b. 1967) in Ghent, Belgium. They all studied at LUCA School of Arts, Faculty of Architecture Campus Ghent. Arúnas left the office in 2007.

NU architectuuratelier is an office for architecture and design research whose ambition is to develop and question spatial projects in collaboration with artists or experts from different fields. By approaching the design process empathically, NU aims to make a qualitative contribution to our social and spatial environment.

NU architectuuratelier has been nominated several times for such national and international prizes as the EU Mies van der Rohe Award (2006 and 2013), the Grand Prix Archizinc Trophy (2006), the Provincial Architecture Prize East Flanders (2007), the Belgian Prize for Architecture and Energy (2013) and the Flemish Monuments Prize (2013).

After his studies, **Armand Eeckels** worked in various architecture firms, including Macken & Macken (Brussels), V+ (Brussels) and evr architecten (Ghent). During his time in the studio of furniture designer and interior architect Maarten Van Severen (Ghent, 1956-2005), he worked with OMA (Rotterdam), among others. He has been a guest lecturer at LUCA School of Arts, Faculty of Architecture in Ghent and Brussels, and at TU Delft (Netherlands).

After his studies, **Halewijn Lievens** worked for Maarten Van Severen, where he supervised architectural projects including the design of the Pont du Gard site in Nîmes (in collaboration with Xaveer De Geyter), the interior design of the Van Abbe Museum in Eindhoven and the competition design for Muziekforum in Ghent in collaboration with OMA (Rotterdam). For four years, he taught at LUCA School of Arts, Faculty of Architecture in Brussels and Ghent.

NU architectuuratelier
Hagelandkaai 50
9000 Ghent, Belgium
www.nuarchitectuuratelier.com

NU architectuuratelier currently includes Aga Batkiewicz, Armand Eeckels, Arthur De Keyser, Charlotte Vyncke, Christoph Foque, Mathilde Geens, Felice Van Tieghem, Francesco Mino, Halewijn Lievens, Jarno Verlinde, Jason Ladrigan, Konstantijn Verbrugge, Olivier Van Calster, Sarah Callewaert and Tim Van Verdegem.

Former collaborators and interns:
Aaron Van Acker, Adya Mittal, Agnieszka Grzemska, Alberto Guisado, Aldo Rooze, Alina Nurmist, Alison Mineau, Anke Schoenmaker, Anne Lise Bouillon, Anouck Tahon, Anthony Leenders, Arian Schelstraete, Arunas Arlauskas, Bert Bogaerts, Bert Stoffels, Bram Lemaire, Carolien Cousserier, Céline Goormachtigh, Charles Dujardin, Christophe Pham, Clément Puech, Daniel van Dijck, Daniela Mikova, Delphine Van Aerde, Diane Estruch, Dora Mathé, Eleonore Devolder, Elise Dupré, Elya Delanote, Emelie Demasure, Eric Van Der Kooij, Esmeralda Bierma, Fien Deruyter, Fran Gómez, Francois Gena, Freek Dendooven, Gabi Hauser, Garance Poëzevara, Giulia Ciuffoletti, Heleen Goethals, Heloïse Bal, Ipek Kosova, Ismael Del Arroyo Vela, Ivana Brzovic, Jochen Schamelhout, Jonathan Teuns, Jonathan Toye, Jose Ignacio Castellitti, Juliette Beaufils, Julija Gindreniene, Junji Koike, Karel Verdonck, Katrien Van Besien, Kristyna Pokojova, Laura Béltran Gonzalez, Laura Vancoillie, Liesa Demuylder, Lieselore Vandecandelaere, Lize Weyenberg, Lonne Deliens, Lore Lambrecht, Louise Vanderlinden, Lucas Renson, Luna Tratsaert, Marie Bemelmans, Marleen Garstenveld, Marnick Beerts, Matteo Lampaert, Matthieu Van Es, Michaela Markova, Minna Vanhoolst, Nathan Heindrichs, Nicolas Deflandre, Nina Bargoin, Pedro de Gois Nogueira, Pieter Vansteeger, Punya Sehmi, Romain Toissaint, Ruth Van de steene, Saar Tilleman, Sander Aelvoet, Sarah Van de Voorde, Sophia Holst, Stefaan Jamaer, Stefan Hooijmans, Sterre Troostheide, Stijn Boon, Szymon Nowakowski, Thomas Veys, Timotheus De Beir, Tom Broekaert, Toon Vercauteren, Trice Hofkens, Valérie Filliers, Willem Broekaert, Yann Courouble, Zareta Shamsadova, Zlatimira Simeonova, Zora Starcevic,…

CREDITS

All images, plans, drawings and sketches: © NU architectuuratelier; unless mentioned otherwise.

Explorations

1, 2, 3, 4 Halvemaanstraat Ghent / 5 35m³ De Singel Antwerp / 6 Kitchen Only, Ghent / 7 Halvemaanstraat Ghent / 8 Zinalrothorn, Switzerland © Koen de Bock / 9 aquarel Bellefroid © Halewijn Lievens / 10 Bellefroid model / 11 From: Jean-Claude Gautrand, *Forteresses du dérisoire* (Les Presses de la Connaissance, 1977) © Philippe Migeat, Centre Pompidou / 12 13 Scheme and visualization from the competition phase (2021 Bellefroid / 14 From: Paul Virilio, Bunker Archeology (2009) © Paul Virilio, *Bunker Archeology* / 15 Skeleton of a sea urchin © Halewijn Lievens / 16, 17 bath © Armand Eeckels & Stefanie Everaert/ 18 bath © Stefanie Everaert / 19 Church of Saint George, Lalibela, Ethiopia, © Ryan Doyle/Video Vision 360 / 20 21 living and gallery space Royden Rabinowitch / 22 Royden Rabinowitch © Isabelle Pateer / 23 Henry Moore, *Helmet Head No.1 1950* (cast 1960) Bronze on wood base © The Henry Moore Foundation / 24 25 26 27 Steinerschool Ghent, competition model and aquarel / 28 Passenger ship on the Mississippi with various decks © Alamy / 29 Kitchen Only, Ghent / 30 31 Temporary tower, Antwerp / 32 33 34 Commandry Gruitrode / 35 Christophe Gerrewey, *50 fictieve gebouwen* (Borgerhoff & Lamberigts, 2014) / 36 Kazimir Malevich, *Black Circle*, oil on canvas, 1915, State Russian Museum, St. Petersburg, Russia. © Public Domain / 37 Crematorium Zemst model / 38 Venice's cemetery on the island of San Michele © creative commons / 39 40 41 Crematorium Zemst plan, visualization and model / 42 Constantin Brancusi, *Le Commencement du monde*, 1920-1924, Centre Pompidou, Paris, Succession Brancusi © Georges Meguerditchian, Centre Pompidou / 43 From: Alice Morse Earle, *Child Life in Colonial Days* (2013) / 44 Cradle bed Huis Perrekes, © Stijn Bollaert / 45 Sculpture in beeswax by Halewijn Lievens © Halewijn Lievens / 46 Rocking chair, the quakers / 47 Still from Ingel Vaikla's film on the cradle bed, 2018 © Ingel Vaikla / 48 49 Testing and assembling the cradle bed at Huis Perrekes © Halewijn Lievens and Esther Goris / 50, 51 cradle bed, research / 52 building a small version of the cradle bed / 53 sketch / 54 Meise Botanic Garden, T- structure / 55 sketch / 56 57 Meise Botanic Garden © Stijn Bollaert / 58 Meise Botanic Garden / 59 Meise Botanic Garden © Stijn Bollaert / 60 61 62 Lierneux, house, sketches, construction site and model / 63 64 65 Windhouse, Shetland Islands / 66 historical maps Windhouse, Shetland Islands / 67 68 69 70 Windhouse model, scheme and plan / 71 Rachel Whiteread, *Vitrine Objects* (2010) © Mike Bruce / 72 Huis Perrekes, furniture / 73 74 Huis Perrekes © Stijn Bollaert / 75 Kitchen Only / 76 77 NU office life / 78 Huis Perrekes, Kings table © Stijn Bollaert / 79 sketch © Halewijn Lievens / 80 81 Huis Perrekes, stillife / 82 Apollo and Dionyus © public domain / 83 84 85 light bricks, plan and sectiondetail, inside and outside drawings / 86 making light bricks, step by step / 87 88 89 light bricks / 90 NU team on trip, campfire / 91 Hannie and Aldo van Eyck, 1947, © J. Versnel, Aldo van Eyck Archives / 92 sketch for a garden bench at Huis Perrekes / 93 94 Water tower, competition visualization and plan / 95 Giant ear trumpet for outer space, U.S. Bell Telephone System's space research laboratory at Holmdel (New Jersey), 1968, © public domain - NASA on the Commons / 96 Listening model, Concertgebouw Brugge, drawing / 97 Listening model, Concertgebouw Brugge © Stijn Bollaert / 98 Listening model, Concertgebouw Brugge / 99 drawing of a piano forte and harpsichord /100 Listening model,

Concertgebouw Brugge, inside machinery and score / 101 close up of a skeleton of a cactus © Shutterstock / 102 The Ark, Botanical Garden Meise, model / 103 The Ark, Botanical Garden Meise, © Stijn Bollaert / 104 105 106 107 The Ark, Botanical Garden Meise, visualization, model in collaboration with Mouton, construction site / 108 C-mine Expedition, Genk © Stijn Bollaert / 109 Close up of a Venus Basket, glass sponge / 110 C-mine Expedition, Genk © Stijn Bollaert / 111 112 C-mine Expedition, Genk, construction site, plan / 113 Huis Perrekes / 114 115 116 117 Noord-Zuid infrastructure Limburg, models, scheme, visualization / 118 119 120 121 Centers, Borgerhout, model, scheme / 122 Centers, Borgerhout, in use © Stijn Bollaert / 123 Centers, Borgerhout, façade / 124 125 Centers, Borgerhout, in use © Stijn Bollaert / 126 Centers, Borgerhout, in use / 127 128 NU team / 129 scheme / 130 ICC - Floraliënhal, Citadelpark, Ghent, plan / 131 Nolli plan / 132 Floraliënhal, Citadelpark, Ghent / 133 Atelier Bouwmeester, Brussels, opening / 134 136 Atelier Bouwmeester, Brussels © Stijn Bollaert / 135 Kasimir Malevich, *Two-Dimensional Self-Portrait*, 1915, © commons / 137 concept image / 138 Concertgebouw Brugge, model / 139 140 Concertgebouw Brugge, © Stijn Bollaert / 141 Concertgebouw Brugge, plan / 142 Concertgebouw Brugge, visualization © Kabvis Mathilde Geens / 143 Concertgebouw Brugge © Stijn Bollaert / 144 Concertgebouw Brugge, guiding spheres / 145 Concertgebouw Brugge © Stijn Bollaert / 146 Jan Van Eyck, *The Annunciation*, 1434 / 147 148 149 150 Wellness, models / 151 J. Duiker and B. Bijvoet, openair school Amsterdam, 1927 / 152 school Waregem, © Stijn Bollaert / 153 154 school Waregem, sketch, collage / 155 156 157 Concertgebouw Brugge, table and lamp, models / 158 Concertgebouw Brugge / 159 The Babe, Lille, lamp / 160 162 Magazine Club, Lille, © Stijn Bollaert / 161 Magazine Club, Lille, plan / 1632 From: *Deceptively Colorful: US Navy Camouflage during World War II* (2020) / 164 165 166 167 Halvemaanstraat, Ghent, shower, sketch, construction / 168 169 170 171 172 B&B, Lierneux, model, plan; construction site / 173 Self-made camp site by Armand Eeckels in the mountains of Guatemala © Armand Eeckels / 174 Fire place Stuk, Ghent, construction / 175 Fire place Stuk, Ghent © Stijn Bollaert / 176 177 178 Picardie, Knokke, construction, model / 179 Picardie, Knokke, stairs © Stijn Bollaert / 180 181 Picardie, Knokke, construction / 182 183 184 185 Picardie, Knokke © Stijn Bollaert / 186 187 C-mine Expedition, Genk / 188 Boxy box, Sint-Martens-Latem, model / 189 translucent panels / 190 frozen waterfall, © Armand Eeckels / 191 192 testing materials / 193 close-up honeycomb / 194 sketch / 195 cutting the honeycomb / 196 in the atelier / 197 translucent panel Boxy pavilion / 198 Table 01 © Stijn Bollaert / 199 200 Table 01, section, drawing / 201 202 Table 01 © Stijn Bollaert / 203 Table 01 in the Linq building © Stijn Bollaert / 204 205 206 Linq, collage and model / 207 208 Linq, Ghent © Stijn Bollaert / 209 210 Linq, Ghent, detail sketch, plan / 211 Bagattenstraat, Ghent, section / 212 Bagattenstraat, Ghent / 213 Bagattenstraat, Ghent © Stijn Bollaert / 214 Bagattenstraat, Ghent, model / 215 Charlotte Rudolph, *Mary Wigman's Dancing Hands*, 1928, © Charlotte Rudolph / 216 217 Bagattenstraat, Ghent © Stijn Bollaert / 218 Bagattenstraat, Ghent, close up / 219 Rachel Whiteread, *Vitrine Objects*, 2009 / 220 Bagattenstraat, Ghent © Stijn Bollaert / 221 Tentoonstellingslaan, Ghent, 2012 © Stijn Bollaert / 222 Haeck house, Sint-Martens-Latem, 2015 © Stijn Bollaert / 223 House Bomastraat, Ghent, 2009 © Stijn

Bollaert / 224 School campus, Waregem, 2019 © Stijn Bollaert / 225 Bar Mother, Lille, 2013 © Stijn Bollaert / 226 NU architectuuratelier office, Ghent / 227 Haeck house, Sint-Martens-Latem, 2015 © Stijn Bollaert / 228 Victoria Theatre, Ghent, 2006 / 229 House Kessel-Lo , 2009 © Stijn Bollaert / 230 stairs Kessel-Lo in atelier / 231 C-mine, Genk, 2012 © Stijn Bollaert / 232 C-mine, Genk, 2012 © Stijn Bollaert / 233 234 235 236 237 238 239 C-mine, Genk, 2012, construction site, models / 241 242 243 C-mine, Genk, 2012 © Stijn Bollaert / 244 245 C-mine, Genk, drawing, construction in the atelier / 246 C-mine, Genk, 2012, plan / 247 C-mine, Genk, 2012 © Stijn Bollaert / 248 crack in earth / 249 250 Ordos, China / 251 252 putting models together, Ordos / 253 254 Ordos, model, plan / 255 256 257 258 Landskouter, 2014, plan, scheme, models / 259 260 261 Zevenbergen, Ranst, model, scheme / 262 263 Zevenbergen, Ranst © Stijn Bollaert / 264 265 266 Emiliani, Zaffelare, model, visualization, drawing / 267 Huis Perrekes, Oosterlo, drawing © Halewijn Lievens / 268 269 Huis Perrekes, Oosterlo © Stijn Bollaert / 270 Huis Perrekes, Oosterlo, construction site / 271 Gordunakaai, Ghent, model / 272 *Napoleon I, Emperor of the French*, Death Mask, The Staatliche Museen' Gipsformerei / 273 274 Gordunakaai, Ghent, model / 275 Photo taken somewhere / 276 Huis Perrekes © Pieter Delbeke / 277 278 Huis Perrekes, Oosterloo / 279 280 281 282 283 Belval, Luxemburg, model, sectiondrawing / 284 Vaartkom, Leuven, competition model / 285 286 287 Pilot project for invisible care, Sint-Truiden, plan, model / 288 schemes / 289 290 291 292 Bracops Hospital, Anderlecht, models, plan / 293 294 295 AZJP Hospital, Vilvoorde, visualization, models / 296 297 UZ Leuven, Campus Gasthuisberg Hospital, models / 298 299 300 UZ Leuven, Campus Gasthuisberg Hospital, models, bench 1 / 301 302 UZ Leuven, Campus Gasthuisberg Hospital, outdoor bench 1 en 2 / 303 Bracops Hospital, Anderlecht, bench / 304 305 306 UZ Leuven, Campus Gasthuisberg Hospital, model and drawing canopy / 307 Dobrava *Floating roof*, Oton Jugovec / 308 Team NU / 309 De Stokkenmanroute, Kattevennen, Genk, testing © Kabvis Mathilde Geens / 310 311 312 313 De Stokkenmanroute, Kattevennen, Genk, drawings and on site / 314 *The Plant Hunter Louis Van Houtte* © FPS Science Policy, on permanent loan to Meise Botanic Garden.

Essay

p. 160 © Stijn Bollaert / p. 161 below © Stijn Bollaert / p. 162 top © Stijn Bollaert / p. 163 © Stijn Bollaert / p. 164 middle © Stijn Bollaert / p. 166 below © Stijn Bollaert / p. 167 © Stijn Bollaert / p. 168 top © Stefan Devoldere / p. 169 below © Stijn Bollaert / p. 171 below © Halewijn Lievens

Portfolio

all images © Stijn Bollaert
except p. 185 : © NU architectuuratelier, p. 210 © Tim Van Verdegem, p. 213 © Sarah Callewaert

The editors and publishers have made every effort to trace and acknowledge copyright holders and secure permission to use copyrighted materials. Any bonafide copyright holder who is not identified or credited here is requested to contact the publihser so that such omission may be rectified in future editions.

COLOPHON

PUBLICATION

Concept
Armand Eeckels, Halewijn Lievens

Editors
Lisa De Visscher, Eline Dehullu, Stefan Devoldere,
Iwan Strauven

Authors
Stefan Devoldere
Lisa De Visscher, Eline Dehullu, Iwan Strauven
Emma Filippides, Ben Rea

Coordination
Eline Dehullu, Mathilde Geens

Research
Armand Eeckels, Arthur De Keyser, Mathilde Geens,
Bertrand Lafontaine, Halewijn Lievens

Cover photography
Stijn Bollaert

English Translation, Proofreading and Copy-editing
Patrick Lennon

Graphic Design and Typesetting
Kabvis (Mathilde Geens)

Publishers
Verlag der Buchhandlung Walther und Franz König (Köln)
A+ Architecture in Belgium (Brussels)
Bozar Books (Brussels)

Printing and Binding
die Keure (Bruges)

Support
The Flemish Authorities

Special thanks to
Arthur De Keyser, Stefan Devoldere, Emma Filippides,
Mathilde Geens, Agnieszka Grzemska, Bertrand
Lafontaine, Francesco Mino, Aldo Rooze, Tim Van
Verdegem

The book size is 210 x 270 cm and its was printed on
Munken Print White paper.
Typefaces: Edita, Raleway, Galano Grotesq

First published by:
Verlag der Buchhandlung Walther und Franz König
Ehrenstraße 4, 50672 Köln
t.: +49 221 20 59 6 53
verlag@buchhandlung-walther-koenig.de
ISBN: 978-3-7533-0512-7

© 2023 NU architectuuratelier (Ghent), the authors,
the photographers, A+ Architecture in Belgium (Brussels),
Bozar (Brussels) and Verlag der Buchhandlung Walther und
Franz König (Köln)

www.nuarchitectuuratelier.com

All rights are reserved. No part of this publication may be
reproduced, stored in a computerized databank, or published or
transmitted in any form or by any means, electronic or mechanical, including photocopying, recording or any other informa-
tion storage or retrieval system, without prior permission in
writing from the publishers. Each author is responsible for his or
her article.

Distribution
Germany, Austria, Switzerland / Europe
Buchhandlung Walther König
Ehrenstraße 4, 50672 Köln
t.: +49 221 20 59 6 53
verlag@buchhandlung-walther-koenig.de

UK and Ireland
Cornerhouse Publications Ltd.
2 Tony Wilson Place, Manchester M15 4FN
t.: +44 161 212 3466
publications@cornerhouse.org

Outside Europe
D.A.P. Distributed Art Publishers, Inc.
75 Broad Street, Suite 630, New York, NY 10004
t.: +1 212 627 1999
orders@dapinc.com

This book was published on the occasion of the
exhibition *NU **architectuuratelier** – Play*, held
from 18.10.2023 to 28.01.2024 at the Centre for
Fine Arts, Brussels (BOZAR).

EXHIBITION:
**NU architectuuratelier
PLAY**

Director of Exhibitions
Zoë Gray

Managerial Head of Exhibitions
Evelyne Hinque

Senior Curatorial Project Coordinators
Ann Flas, Anne Judong

Concept
Armand Eeckels, Halewijn Lievens

Curators
Lisa De Visscher, Lara Molino, Iwan Strauven

Coordination
Lara Molino (A+)
Arthur De Keyser, Sarah Callewaert (NU)

Exhibition Design
NU architectuuratelier (Armand Eeckels,
Halewijn Lievens, Arthur De Keyser, Sarah Callewaert)
ABC Art Basics for Children (Gerhard Jäger)

Film Explorations
Bertrand Lafontaine

Photography
Stijn Bollaert

Models
NU architectuuratelier

Technical Head of Production
Fred Oulieu assisted by Gert Baart

Lighting
Colin Fincoeur

Assistant to the Director of Exhibitions
Axelle Ancion

Audience Development
Thomas Vandemeulebroucke, Loes Van Hoof

Press
Barbara Porteman

Co-production
Centre for Fine Arts, Brussels (BOZAR)
A+ Architecture in Belgium

Support
The Flemish Authorities

A+ Architecture in Belgium

Chair of the Board of Directors: Philémon Wachtelaer
Artistic Direction: Lisa De Visscher
Publications: Eline Dehullu
Exhibitions and lectures: Lara Molino, Mattijs Brandt
Production and IT: Grégoire Maus
Office Management and subscriptions: Deborah Schwarzbaum
Communication and Press: Louise Van Laethem, Maude Huyberechts
Advertising and sponsoring: Rita Minissi

Centre for Fine Arts, Brussels (BOZAR)

Chief Executive Officer – Artistic Director: Christophe Slagmuylder
Chief Operations Officer: Albert Wastiaux
Finance Director: Christine Perpette
Exhibitions Director: Zoë Gray
Music Director: Jérôme Giersé
Marketing & Communication Director: Marianne Janssens
Human Resources Director: Ignace De Breuck
Head of Cinema: Juliette Duret
Head of Artistic Development A.I.: Evelyne Hinque
Head of Institutional Relations: Magdalena Liskova
Head of Partnerships & Philanthropy: Elke Kristoffersen
Managerial Head of Exhibitions: Evelyne Hinque
Audience Engagement Manager: Tine Van Goethem
Planning Manager & Ticketing: Annik Halmes
Public Services Manager: Matthieu Vanderdonckt
ICT & Digital Manager: François Pettiaux
Investments, Security & Archives Manager: Stéphane Vanreppelen
Manager Cleaning & Stock: Rudi Anneessens
Maintenance Manager: Eduardo Oblanca
Production Manager: Nicolas Bernus

With the thankful support of our sponsors: